Life in the THIRTEEN COLONIES

Maryland

Michael Burgan

children's press®
An imprint of
SCHOLASTIC

Library of Congress Cataloging-in-Publication Data

Burgan, Michael.
  Maryland / by Michael Burgan.
      p. cm. — (Life in the thirteen colonies)
  Includes bibliographical references and index.
  ISBN 0-516-24571-6
  1. Maryland—History—Colonial period, ca. 1600–1775—Juvenile literature. 2. Maryland—History—
1775–1865—Juvenile literature. I. Title. II. Series.
  F184.B885 2004
  975.2'02—dc22
                                    2004009549

1 2 3 4 5 6 7 8 9 10 R 13 12 11 10 09 08 07 06 05 04

A Creative Media Applications Production
Design: Fabia Wargin Design
Production: Alan Barnett, Inc.
Editor: Matt Levine
Copy Editor: Laurie Lieb
Proofreader: Tania Bissell
Content Research: Lauren Thogersen
Photo Researcher: Annette Cyr
Content Consultant: David Silverman, Ph.D.

Photo Credits © 2004

Cover: Top left © North Wind Archives; Top right © Bettmann/CORBIS; Bottom left © Getty Images/Hulton Archive;
Bottom right © North Wind Archives; Background © Getty Images/Hulton Archive; Title page © Getty Images/Hulton
Archive; p. 2 © North Wind Archives; p. 6 © North Wind Archives; p. 10 © North Wind Archives; p. 15 ©
Bettmann/CORBIS; p. 16 © North Wind Archives; p. 22 © North Wind Archives; p. 24 © North Wind Archives; p. 27 ©
Getty Images/Hulton Archive; p. 30 © North Wind Archives; p. 34 © Getty Images/Hulton Archive; p. 39 © North Wind
Archives; p. 40 © Bettmann/CORBIS; p. 42 © North Wind Archives; p. 45 © North Wind Archives; p. 47 © Getty
Images/Hulton Archive; p. 48 © North Wind Archives; p. 51 © North Wind Archives; p. 52 © North Wind Archives; p. 55 ©
North Wind Archives; p. 58 © Paul A. Souders/CORBIS; p. 60: Left top © Peter Finger/CORBIS; Right top © Richard T.
Nowitz/CORBIS; Left bottom © William A. Bake/CORBIS; Right middle © Angelo Hornak/CORBIS; Right bottom ©
North Wind Archives; p. 61: Left top © Michael Freeman/CORBIS; Right top © Richard T. Nowitz/CORBIS; Right bottom
© Lee Snider; Lee Snider/CORBIS; p. 62 © Getty Images/Hulton Archive; p. 64 © Getty Images/Hulton Archive; p. 67 ©
CORBIS; p. 69 © Getty Images/Hulton Archive; p. 76 © North Wind Archives; p. 78 © North Wind Archives; p. 85 © North
Wind Archives; p. 87 © North Wind Archives; p. 88 © North Wind Archives; p. 93 © North Wind Archives; p. 94 © Getty
Images/Hulton Archive; p. 96 © North Wind Archives; p. 101 © CORBIS; p. 104 © Bettmann/CORBIS; p. 106 © CORBIS;
p. 108 © Bettmann/CORBIS; p. 111 © Bettmann/CORBIS; p. 112 © North Wind Archives; p. 118: Top left © North Wind
Archives; Top right © North Wind Archives; Bottom left © North Wind Archives; Bottom right © Paul A. Souders/CORBIS;
p. 119: Top left © Getty Images/Hulton Archive; Top right © Bettmann/CORBIS; Bottom © Bettmann/CORBIS; Background
© North Wind Archives

CONTENTS

THE
ORIGINAL
THIRTEEN COLONIES,
1775

NEW FRANCE

MAINE
(part of
Mass.)

St. Lawrence River
Lake
Champlain

Lake Ontario

NEW
HAMPSHIRE

• Falmouth

Portsmouth
• Newburyport
Salem •
Boston •

MASSACHUSETTS

Lake Erie

Mohawk R.
Albany •

NEW YORK

Connecticut River
Hudson R.

Cape
Cod

Hartford •

Newport •

New Haven •

RHODE ISLAND
CONNECTICUT

Delaware R.

Appalachian Mountains

Susquehanna R.

New York •

Long
Island

PENNSYLVANIA

Philadelphia •

Perth Amboy

Pittsburgh •

York •

• Burlington

NEW JERSEY

Baltimore •

• New Castle

Ohio River

Potomac R.

MARYLAND

DELAWARE

Alexandria •

Atlantic
Ocean

Chesapeake Bay

James River Richmond •

• Williamsburg

VIRGINIA

• Norfolk

Roanoke River

Edenton •

Hillsboro •   Halifax •

Cape
Hatteras

Salem •
NORTH CAROLINA   Bath •
New Bern •

Pamlico
Sound

Salisbury •

• Charlotte

Cross
Creek

Cape Fear R.

Camden •

• Wilmington

SOUTH
CAROLINA

Savannah River

• Georgetown

Augusta •

GEORGIA

Charles Town •

Savannah •

SPANISH TERRITORY

Legend

——— Colonial boundaries
(The western boundaries of many
colonies were undefined in 1775.)

0   125   250

Scale in Miles

A Nation Grows
From Thirteen Colonies

Maryland lies in the mid-Atlantic region of the United States. It was one of the original thirteen colonies. Maryland is bordered by Pennsylvania on the north, Virginia on the west and south, and Delaware on the east. Part of its eastern border is formed by the Atlantic Ocean.

Chesapeake Bay, located in the center of the state, has shaped Maryland's history for thousands of years. Before Europeans discovered its rich fishing grounds, Native Americans lived along the shore of the bay. English colonists arrived in the 1600s. They settled on the banks of the Chesapeake and created a new colony.

The history of Maryland colony is the story of people seeking freedom. These included slaves who were brought to the colony by force, religious groups, and colonists fighting for freedom from English rule.

⌐ The map shows the thirteen English colonies in 1775. The colored sections show the areas that were settled at that time.

CHAPTER ONE

Europeans in the New World

Exploring the Chesapeake

In May 1498, John Cabot left Bristol, England, with five ships. Cabot, who was originally from Italy, was leading a voyage of exploration. On this journey, he became the first European to sail into Chesapeake Bay. His ships passed by Maryland's eastern shore.

Cabot claimed the land he saw for England's King Henry VII. But Cabot never returned to England. All but one of his ships mysteriously disappeared. Today, no one knows the details of his trip.

Twenty years later, Cabot's son Sebastian made his own **expedition** to the New World. (Europeans considered Europe the Old World. They called North and South America the New World.) Some historians say that he,

⊲ John Cabot convinced British merchants to pay for his voyage of discovery. Cabot's real name was Giovanni Caboto.

not his father, may have really been the first European to actually see the shores of Maryland.

For several decades, Europeans largely ignored Chesapeake Bay and the lands around it. Then, in 1524, Giovanni da Verrazano explored the Atlantic coast of North America. This Italian captain was sailing for King Francis I of France. Verrazano passed by Chesapeake Bay. He landed briefly on a **peninsula** that borders the bay.

Verrazano met some of the Native Americans who lived in the region. In a letter to King Francis, Verrazano said that their food had "a very delicious flavor." He also noted that they sailed "boats made of one tree 20 feet [6 meters] long and four feet [1.2 meters] broad."

The Indians of the Chesapeake

The people Verrazano met most likely belonged to an Algonquian tribe. At the time, Native Americans who spoke the Algonquian language stretched from what would one day be eastern Canada to the Carolinas. The Algonquian lived on both the eastern and western shores of the bay.

The Eastern Shore tribes included the Tockwogh, Wicomiss, Choptank, Nanticoke, and Pocomoke. Across the bay lived the Piscataway, Mattawoman, Patuxent, Yaocomaco, and several other tribes. As least 12,000 people lived along Chesapeake Bay when Europeans first landed there.

Most Algonquian families of the Chesapeake lived in wigwams. These dome-shaped homes were made of bark that covered wooden frames. A hole in the center of the roof let in light and let out smoke from a fire in the middle of the room. For large gatherings, tribal members met in bigger structures called long-houses. These buildings were also made out of wood and bark and had rounded roofs. Many Algonquian communities ringed their wigwams and longhouses with high wooden fences called palisades. These fences kept out enemies.

Maryland's Indians lived in small villages near water, close to the forests they needed to survive. Trees provided fuel for their fires and wood for homes and tools. The men of a village hunted forest animals, using bows and arrows. Their game included deer, bears, squirrels, and turkeys. Besides food, the animals provided furs and skins that were used for clothes. Women and children gathered nuts from the trees, and berries that grew wild in nearby fields.

What's in a Name?

———～⁓❁⁓～———

The peninsula where Verrazano landed is today called the Delmarva Peninsula. *Delmarva* comes from letters in the names of the three states that share the peninsula— Delaware, Maryland, and Virginia.

Fish and Farm

The forest was not the only important resource for the Algonquian. Chesapeake Bay and the rivers that flowed into it were also a major source of food. The bay got its name from the many fish living in it. *Chesapeake* is an Algonquian word meaning "great shellfish bay." In these waters lived plump oysters and other shellfish. The Indians also fished for bass and caught turtles called diamond-backed terrapins.

The shores and waters of Chesapeake Bay were the main sources of food for the Algonquian Indian tribes that lived in Maryland.

To travel on the water, Algonquian fishers made canoes such as the ones Verrazano saw. A single large tree was hollowed out to make a canoe. To do this, the canoe builders set the tree on fire. Then they scraped out the burned, blackened wood with shells or wooden hand tools.

The Maryland tribes had once survived on just wild animals and plants. Around A.D. 1,000, they began to raise crops on a large scale. Men cleared the fields, and women did the planting and farming. Both women and children sometimes sat on wooden platforms above the fields. From there, they scared away birds that tried to eat the crops. Families also raised food in small gardens near their homes.

The Algonquian's main crops were corn, beans, and squash. They called these three crops the "Three Sisters." Beans provided protein, which humans need to live. They also added nitrogen to the soil. This fertilizer helped the other crops grow. Corn was especially valuable. The kernels were ground into a flour that fed both people and animals. The husks, which cover the corn ears, could be used to stuff chairs or beds.

The Algonquian also raised tobacco. They used this plant as a medicine and smoked it during religious ceremonies. After English settlers reached Maryland, tobacco became their leading crop.

The Algonquian tribes of Maryland sometimes traded with each other and with distant tribes. Traders carried their goods along paths cut through the woods or sailed in their canoes up and down rivers and streams. For money, the Algonquian and other Native Americans of the East used strings of colorful beads called wampum. The beads were made from the shells of clams and other shellfish. Wampum was also made into belts on which the beads were arranged into patterns. The patterns usually stood for a tribe's important religious and political ideas.

Indian Leaders

A typical Algonquian community had several important leaders. Five or six tribes sometimes joined together to form a larger group, called a **confederacy**.

Each tribe had local chiefs, called *werowances*. They decided when the tribes went to war and which land tribal members would farm. *Werowances* also settled disputes among tribal members, greeted guests to their villages, and advised the *tayac* (head chief). The *werowances* had their own advisers who helped them run tribal affairs. The power to rule as a *werowance* was usually passed on to a male relative. Rarely, an Algonquian tribe might have a female leader.

Working with the Indians' leaders were shamans. The tribes believed that these religious figures had special powers that let them communicate with spirits. Across North America, Native Americans believed that the world was filled with unseen spirits. All living things had spirits that survived after death. Spirits also shaped weather, bringing damaging storms or blistering heat. Some spirits were helpful, while others were evil. Through chants and dancing, shamans entered the spirit world, where they received the power to heal the sick or predict the future. They brought that power with them when they returned to the world of humans.

A Region Called Virginia

Verrazano stayed only briefly on the Chesapeake Peninsula. He and his crew did not upset the lives of the Indians who lived there. This was not true of other Europeans who explored the Chesapeake in decades that followed. From 1561 to 1572, the Spanish sent several expeditions to Maryland. After a few bloody battles with the Algonquian, the Spanish left the Chesapeake for good. They decided to concentrate on their colonies further south, in the Carolinas and Florida.

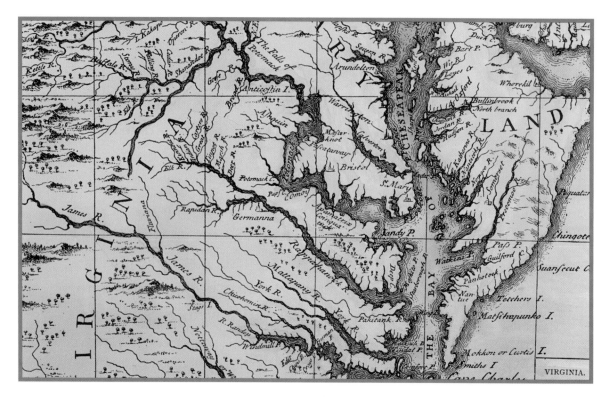

This early map shows the many fingers of Chesapeake Bay stretching north from Virginia into what would become the colony of Maryland.

The Spanish had competition in the Carolinas. Both France and England tried to colonize that part of the New World. In 1587, Sir Walter Raleigh organized a group of about 100 English settlers. They landed at Roanoke Island, in what is now North Carolina. The English called the area Virginia. This region stretched along the Atlantic coast from present-day northern Florida to Nova Scotia, Canada. Within four years, all the settlers at Roanoke had mysteriously disappeared. Historians sometimes call Roanoke "the Lost Colony."

Despite that failure, in 1607 the English sent another expedition to Virginia. About 100 settlers arrived on three ships and built a fort along a river. They named their settlement Jamestown, after their king, James I. The English struggled to survive in their new colony, battling starvation, harsh weather, and disease.

The colonists also sometimes fought with the local tribes. The Algonquian of the region belonged to the Powhatan Confederacy. The Powhatan distrusted the English and Europeans in general. In the past, the Spanish had sometimes forced Indians into slavery or stolen their lands.

One of the English leaders at Jamestown was John Smith. Brave and bold, he took part in some of the disputes that led to bloodshed between the Powhatan and the settlers. He also explored Chesapeake Bay, as well as several rivers in Maryland. He wrote that Indian farms along the Potomac River produced "plenty and variety of fruit."

The Susquehannock

Smith's adventures took him into the northern part of Chesapeake Bay. That region was the home of the Susquehannock. This Indian tribe was not part of the Algonquian group. It was related to the Iroquois tribes of New York and Pennsylvania. The Susquehannock lived along the Susquehanna River. This river flows from New York through eastern Pennsylvania and into Chesapeake Bay.

The Susquehannock brought Smith and his men gifts, including deer meat, tobacco, and weapons. Although the Susquehannock were kind to the English, they had bad relations with the Algonquian Indians. The Susquehannock sometimes journeyed from their villages in present-day Pennsylvania to attack Algonquian villages. The Algonquian feared their fierce battle skills. The Susquehannock would force other tribes to move to new lands and take their hunting territory and possessions.

The Susquehannock did not bother the English settlers in Jamestown, but the Powhatan did. In 1622, the Native Americans realized that the colonists were not going away and would continue to take their land. An Indian attack on Jamestown killed more than 300 colonists.

Over the next decade, the English responded with their own raids. They drove the Powhatan and other Algonquian tribes off their homelands. Indians in what would become Maryland also felt the blast of English guns and the deep cut of English swords.

During this long struggle with the Powhatan, the Susquehannock and the English had peaceful relations. William Claiborne and other English settlers traded with the Susquehannock. Claiborne traded such goods as metal tools, glass, and guns for beaver fur. In Europe, soft, warm beaver fur was prized for hats and other clothing. Europeans had traded with Native Americans for this valuable fur since the sixteenth century.

As more Europeans craved beaver fur, its price rose. Over time, French traders won control of the beaver trade. Claiborne wanted to take some of their business. He hoped the Susquehannock's ties to other Indians across the Northeast would help his fur trade.

William Claiborne's settlement on Kent Island would become part of Maryland colony.

In 1631, Claiborne set up a fort on an island in Chesapeake Bay. He named the island for the English county, Kent, where he was born. Kent Island is near what is now Annapolis, the capital of Maryland. Claiborne's small colony was the first English settlement in what became Maryland. But at the time, Kent Island was still considered part of Virginia.

Within a few years, about a hundred people lived on the island. Claiborne was making a good living with his fur trade. His and other fur traders' success drew the attention of **investors** and aristocrats (people of power and wealth) in England. Seeing how much money the colonists were making, the investors wanted to start their own businesses in Virginia.

George Calvert

One of the men who wanted to start a business in the New World was George Calvert, the first Lord Baltimore. He had held several government positions in England and was friends with King James I. Just before James died in 1625, he made Calvert a baron. This position among the British **nobility** allowed Calvert to be addressed by the title "Lord." With this title, Calvert could sit in **Parliament**. Parliament was the governing body that made England's laws. Calvert's title would pass to his eldest son.

George Calvert, the first Lord Baltimore, was the founder of Maryland. When he died, his son Cecilius became the second Lord Baltimore.

Like most barons, Calvert was wealthy. He was one of the investors in the company that had founded the settlement at Jamestown. Although that colony had struggled to make money, Calvert still thought he could make a great fortune in North America.

In 1620, Calvert had bought land in Newfoundland, Canada. Two years later, King James let him start a colony there. When Calvert visited Newfoundland in 1627, he found the "air so intolerable cold as it is hardly to be endured." The bitter weather convinced Calvert that he could never build a successful colony there. In 1629, he sailed to Virginia, looking for better land for a new colony. The Jamestown settlers did not welcome him warmly. Calvert was a Roman Catholic, while the Virginians were Protestants.

In Europe, Protestants and Catholics had battled each other for almost a century. Each side disliked the other's religious beliefs. When Protestants came to power, they usually limited what Catholics could do. Catholics did the same thing to Protestants. In seventeenth-century England, Protestants controlled the government. They denied Catholics the freedom to worship in public or hold government jobs. The Protestant **prejudice** against Catholics thrived in the New World. By one report, a Jamestown settler threatened to beat up Calvert because of his faith.

Calvert's Colony

Despite his treatment in Virginia, Calvert wanted to start a colony in the region. He took a trip up Chesapeake Bay and saw land north of Jamestown. He later wrote that the land was "fit to be the home of a happy people." Charles I, the son of James I, was now king. Calvert asked Charles to give him the land he had seen along the Chesapeake.

Calvert drew up a charter. This legal document spelled out his rights and duties in his American lands. Calvert would own the land and could sell it or give it away. He and his heirs would also govern the colony as they chose. One historian wrote that, in theory, Calvert would have "a greater power…than did the king in England." Yet the settlers had some political rights. The charter guaranteed that they or their elected officials had to approve the colony's laws.

In June 1632, Charles approved Calvert's charter. The king called the new colony Maryland, naming it for his queen, Henrietta Maria. In return for the land, Calvert was supposed to pay Charles two Indian arrowheads every Easter. He also had to give the king 20 percent of any gold or silver he found.

Why Baltimore

In 1621, King James rewarded George Calvert for his loyal service. The king gave him land in Ireland. For some reason, Calvert called his lands Baltimore. Ireland has a town of the same name, but Calvert had no known connection to it. King James then made Calvert the Baron of Baltimore. This led to his title Lord Baltimore, which he passed down to his sons. It also became the name of Maryland's major city.

The deal was a bargain for Calvert, but he never enjoyed life in his new lands. He died two months before Charles gave his final approval of the charter. The charter then passed to Calvert's son Cecilius, the second Lord Baltimore. Cecilius would carry out his father's wishes to make Maryland a successful colony.

MARYLAND,
1775

Appalachian Mountains

PENNSYLVANIA

Susquehanna River

Fort Cumberland

NEW
JERSEY

MARYLAND

Monocacy River

Potomac River

Frederick
Town

Patapsco River

Baltimore

Patuxent R.

DELAWARE

Annapolis

Kent
Island

VIRGINIA

St. Clement's
Bay

St. Mary's
City

Chesapeake
Peninsula

St. Clement's
Island

Chesapeake Bay

NORTH

WEST   EAST

SOUTH

Atlantic
Ocean

Legend

Colonial boundaries
(The western boundaries of many
colonies were undefined in 1775.)

0   25
Scale in Miles

CHAPTER TWO
Founding a Colony

Two Faiths

For more than a year, Cecilius Calvert **recruited** settlers willing to make the long, dangerous voyage across the Atlantic Ocean. He placed his younger brother Leonard in charge of the expedition. On November 22, 1633, the ships *Ark* and *Dove* left England.

The 150 or so passengers on the two ships were both Catholics and Protestants. Lord Baltimore hoped that the members of the two faiths could peacefully live and work together in his colony. He hoped they would not carry their prejudices to the New World.

Lord Baltimore wanted the Catholics in his colony to avoid angering the Protestants near them. He instructed the Catholic colonists to practice their religion "as privately as may be" and "to be silent…concerning matters of religion."

This map shows how Maryland looked in 1775.

Still, he let Catholic **missionaries** sail with the colonists. Their goal was to teach the Catholic faith to Maryland's Native Americans.

Some Protestants in England and Virginia had opposed the Calverts' charter. They feared that Maryland would become a center for the Roman Catholic Church in America. Since he knew he had enemies who opposed his colony, Lord Baltimore stayed in England. There, he could make sure that Protestants did not try to take away his land or limit his rights as proprietor.

Voyage and Arrival

One of the missionaries to Maryland was a Catholic priest named Andrew White. Father White kept a detailed diary of the voyage across the Atlantic and the settlers' first experiences in Maryland. In his diary, White described several fierce storms. During one storm, he wrote, the passengers "were in fear of imminent death all this night." But for most of the trip, the *Ark* and the *Dove* sailed on smooth waters.

After crossing the Atlantic, the ships made a few stops at islands in the Caribbean Sea. In February 1634, the *Ark* and the *Dove* sailed into Chesapeake Bay. The colonists spent some time in Virginia before finally reaching Lord Baltimore's lands.

On March 25, the two ships anchored at a small island. The colonists named it St. Clement's. Leonard Calvert then kept sailing in the *Dove* to meet the Indians of the region. He wanted to assure them that the colonists were friendly.

Sailing with Calvert was Henry Fleet, a Virginian who had traded with the Algonquian of the Chesapeake. Because he knew the Indians' language and customs, he acted as Calvert's guide. Within several days, Calvert bought land from the Yaocomaco Indians. He paid them with cloth and metal tools, such as axes and hoes. Calvert then named the new settlement St. Mary's City, and it became Maryland's first capital. The Maryland Assembly, the colony's body of elected lawmakers, met there for the first time in 1635. Leonard Calvert served as Maryland's first governor.

A View of Maryland

Father White's writings gave the English one of their first descriptions of Maryland's natural beauty. He called Chesapeake Bay "the most delightful water I ever saw." The soil in Maryland, he said, was excellent, "so that we cannot set down a foot, but tread on strawberries...acorns, walnuts, sassafras, etc: and those in the wildest woods." The forests, White added, were filled with "delicate springs, which are our best drink," and in the skies flew eagles, swans, geese, and ducks. "The place abounds not alone with profit," White wrote, "but also with pleasure."

The Marylanders had an advantage as they started their colony. They had learned from the mistakes that the Virginia settlers had made in Jamestown. Calvert had planned his trip across the Atlantic so the settlers would arrive in the spring. They would have time to grow enough crops for their first winter. Calvert also knew he needed peaceful relations with the Native Americans, which is why he asked Fleet for help. The Marylanders began planting tobacco right away, giving them a valuable crop they could sell in England.

Cecilius Calvert, the second Lord Baltimore, established friendly relations with the local Indians in Maryland.

Early Troubles

Maryland's biggest problems came from William Claiborne and other Virginians. Claiborne refused to accept that Kent Island was part of Lord Baltimore's colony. He also saw the Marylanders as a threat to his fur trade. In April 1634, he tried to convince the Susquehannock to attack a Maryland boat. Later, Claiborne spread the rumor that the new settlers were actually from Spain. He knew that the Algonquian of the region hated the Spanish. Claiborne's efforts, however, failed to stir the Indians against Calvert and his colonists.

Calvert and the other colonists knew that Claiborne could not be trusted. They also thought his business on Kent Island harmed their efforts to trade with the Indians. In London, England's capital, Lord Baltimore arranged for Virginia to shut down Claiborne's business.

Claiborne responded in 1635 by arming several ships and attacking boats from St. Mary's City. Some historians have called these conflicts the first naval battles in American waters. Claiborne finally left Kent Island in 1637. Still, he continued to support Lord Baltimore's enemies in attempts to destroy the Maryland colony.

New troubles began in 1642. The Susquehannock attacked the settlers and the Piscataway. A few years later, Claiborne returned to the region and used troops from

The battle between Claiborne's and Calvert's ships was the first naval conflict on Chesapeake Bay.

Virginia to attack Maryland. This militia (group of citizen soldiers) claimed that Lord Baltimore and Governor Calvert held "**tyrannical** power against the Protestants."

Shortly before his death in 1647, Governor Calvert led a counterattack against the Virginia forces. The next year, Lord Baltimore named William Stone, a Virginia Protestant, as governor. Baltimore realized that he needed Protestant support and allies in Virginia for his colony to survive. He also wanted more Protestants to settle in Maryland. One way was to appoint a Protestant governor.

Another way to get Protestant support was to ensure that their religious rights were protected.

In 1649, the Assembly passed "A Law of Maryland Concerning Religion." The law let Roman Catholics and Protestants worship as they chose, without any restrictions. Non-Christians, such as Jews, did not receive this legal protection. The act was the first law passed in America granting religious freedom to all Christians.

Farming in a New Land

Maryland's first settlers hoped they would make money trading for furs. Soon, however, they turned to farming to meet their needs. The colonists, like the Native Americans, relied on corn as their main food crop at first. They also borrowed the Indians' farming methods. The settlers usually did not cut down trees to clear their farmlands. Instead, they scraped the bark off the trees close to the ground. This process, called girdling, stopped sap from flowing. As the sap dried up, the trees' leaves and upper branches died. The farmers then planted seeds in small hills around the bare trees, where sunlight could now easily reach the ground.

Tobacco was the major crop in Maryland, as it was in neighboring Virginia. Almost everyone who owned land planted tobacco, and for a time it served as the colony's money. People paid their debts and bought goods in pounds of the leafy plant.

Growing tobacco was hard work. Farmers had to constantly remove weeds that grew near the plants and kill bugs that ate them. When the plants were ripe, they had to be cut and then dried.

The farmers stored and transported tobacco in huge barrels called hogsheads. Each one held several hundred pounds of tobacco. Farmers rolled the hogsheads to docks where boats and ships waited to bring the crop to market. It made sense to start a **plantation** as close to the docks as possible. Planters who were not close to the water cut paths through forests and fields. Then they rolled their hogsheads to the nearest docks.

Tobacco required rich soil. After a few growing seasons, the farmland became less fertile, or able to grow crops. When this happened, farmers simply moved on to new fields. The land they left behind could not be used again unless farmers added **fertilizers**.

Life was hard on the typical Maryland farm. People often rose before sunrise to start their chores and worked until sunset. During the short days of winter, they might do some of their chores by the light of lanterns. Life in early Maryland could also be dangerous. The warm, humid climate of a Chesapeake summer was perfectly suited for mosquitoes. The insects carried diseases, such as malaria and yellow fever. Mosquito bites could pass these diseases to humans.

Malaria was the most common disease of the time. It did not usually kill people, but it weakened their health. After catching malaria, settlers often caught other illnesses that could kill, such as the flu.

The settlers were most likely to die from disease when they first arrived. This period was called the "seasoning"

Maryland tobacco was put into barrels called hogsheads and shipped to Europe for sale.

time. People who survived their first months in Maryland were "seasoned." But even seasoned settlers faced a short lifespan. During Maryland's first decades, settlers were lucky to live past the age of forty.

Attracting Settlers

To make money with his colony, Lord Baltimore needed to attract as many settlers as possible. He promised to give land to people who moved to Maryland. A person who paid for himself and five workers to cross the Atlantic received 2,000 acres (810 hectares). Settlers with less money received 100 acres (41 hectares) of land. They got extra land for bringing a family and servants with them. Most of Maryland's first farms covered about 125 acres (51 hectares).

The harsh conditions in Maryland did not attract many men with families, or many single women. During most of the seventeenth century, Maryland had three or four men for every woman who settled there. Some males, desperate for brides, married girls as young as twelve years old.

Married women had no legal and political rights. They were expected to work hard in the tobacco fields, as well as raise families. They were considered their husbands' property. Single women and widows had some rights, since they could own property. Widows sometimes took over their dead husbands' farms or businesses. But on the whole, women were not considered equal to men.

The legal system reflected this belief. Having a child before marriage was illegal, but usually only the woman was punished for this crime. One seventeenth-century writer recorded that one unwed mother was "carried to the public whipping post and there to have thirty lashes well laid upon her bare back by the sheriff."

Ahead of Her Time

Margaret Brent was a rare exception in colonial Maryland. Never married, she acted independently of her male relatives in business and legal affairs. Brent came from a wealthy Catholic family, and both she and her sister Mary owned property. Margaret loaned money to new settlers and recruited workers to come to the colony. She was also close to Leonard Calvert. He gave her the legal power to represent his interests after his death. In effect, she was the governor's attorney, making her the first female lawyer in North America. Brent took charge of Calvert's affairs during a difficult time. When he died in 1647, Maryland owed its militia money. Brent made sure that the soldiers were fed and paid. The next year, Brent asked the Assembly to let her vote, but it said no. At that time, women were not allowed to vote or hold elected office. Still, Brent had taken a bold step in supporting legal rights for women in Maryland.

Slaves

In Great Britain and its colonies, free white men controlled society. Most people believed that white men were superior to women and nonwhite people. Even within the class of white men, distinct layers of society developed. Wealthy and powerful aristocrats were considered better than merchants or **artisans**. Plantation owners were better than the hired workers who raised their crops. Everyone was said to have a distinct place in society. People had to respect and obey the people above them.

With these attitudes, English society easily accepted slavery. Most Europeans of the time thought that the dark-

During the mid-1600s, Maryland farmers started using slaves from Africa and the Caribbean to work on their farms.

skinned people of Africa were inferior to whites. The Europeans did not hesitate to turn the Africans into slaves. The Africans were used to living and working in steamy tropical climates. Many of the first New World colonies, especially those in the Caribbean, were equally hot and humid. The Europeans believed that the African slaves could survive the conditions better than other workers could.

At the end of the fifteenth century, the European country of Portugal began buying slaves in West Africa. It transported the slaves to the New World and sold them in European colonies in the Caribbean and North America. Over the next three centuries, the growth of European colonies in the New World fueled a boom in the slave trade.

In the British colonies of North America, including Maryland, colonists first used Native Americans as slaves. Over time, however, black African slaves became more common. Records show that in 1642, Leonard Calvert purchased seventeen slaves. These might have been the colony's first African slaves.

First African

The first Marylander of African descent was Mathias de Sousa. He was half white and half African. People with mixed racial backgrounds such as his were called **mulattoes**. De Sousa came on the *Ark* as an indentured servant. Once he received his freedom, he worked as a sailor, fur trader, and politician.

Slavery existed for several decades before the Maryland Assembly officially legalized it in 1664. A law passed that year said that any slaves brought into the colony remained slaves for life. Their children were also slaves for life. Maryland was the first American colony to pass this kind of slave law. St. Mary's City eventually became a slave-trading port. Planters went there to buy slaves who arrived on ships from Africa or British colonies in the West Indies.

Indentured Servants

During Maryland's early years, indentured servants were much more common than slaves. Planters or merchants agreed to pay for the servants' passage from Europe to America and give them food, shelter, and clothing. In return, the servants worked for their masters for a number of years. The typical period was five to seven years. The contract that both masters and servants signed was called an indenture.

Indentured servants lived with their masters. They could not own property or travel without their masters' permission. For most servants, entering into this contract was the only way they

Freedom Dues

By law, masters had to help indentured servants adjust to life after their service was done. The servants received what were called "freedom dues." Their masters gave them such things as clothes, tobacco, corn, tools, and their own land to farm.

could afford to come to America. They accepted a certain loss of freedom, hoping they could make a good living when their service ended. For merchants and planters, indentured servants provided cheap labor. That labor was important, since Maryland lacked enough workers to run its economy.

Some indentured servants were skilled artisans (craftspeople), such as carpenters or tailors. Even teachers could be servants. Most, however, were young, unskilled Englishmen who sweated in the tobacco fields. Some Africans also came to Maryland as indentured servants. Later in the seventeenth century, women, children, and convicts joined the ranks of servants. Women often worked in the master's home, because the English did not think that farming was "women's work." But when farm workers were scarce, the women joined the men in the fields.

On small farms, masters and servants lived similar lives. Robert Beverly, an early historian of Virginia and Maryland, wrote that "the work of…servants and slaves is no other than what every common **freeman** does."

By law, masters had to give their servants "sufficient" food, clothing, and housing. Servants could take their masters to court if they were treated unfairly. Some masters beat their indentured servants, and the servants might run away to escape this abuse. Still, most indentured servants believed that their new lives in Maryland were better than the ones they left behind.

CHAPTER THREE

Building a Colony

Growing Slowly

Maryland's population grew slowly during the mid-seventeenth century. The shortage of women prevented men from marrying and starting families. The colony relied on **immigration** to increase its population. Some immigrants came from Virginia. Most of the new arrivals were indentured servants from England. In general, planters recruited new servants when tobacco prices were high. The planters wanted to grow as much of the crop as possible during those good times, and they needed more labor to do it.

A Planter's Life

Planters usually sold their tobacco crops themselves once they were harvested. They did not rely on merchants to do it for them. Small farmers might sell their crop to large plantation

↪ *Growing tobacco was very hard work, but it was the main crop for most Maryland farmers.*

owners. These wealthier planters could bring the crop to market easier than small farmers could. Successful farmers had to be skillful both on the soil and in the marketplace.

At first, all tobacco farmers were called planters. Over time, however, the title was usually given only to the men who owned large plantations. Maryland's society and politics were eventually controlled by these wealthy planters. During the colony's early years, however, most planters were not rich. Some did not even own the land they farmed. Instead, they rented it from wealthier planters. In some cases, freemen worked for wages on someone else's farm.

Attracting Immigrants

The Calverts tried to encourage people to settle in Maryland. By 1666, Charles Calvert, the third Lord Baltimore, was the proprietor of Maryland. He used a **pamphlet** that described life in Maryland to attract new settlers. *A Character of the Province of Maryland* was written by George Alsop, a former indentured servant. He wrote, "Maryland abounds in a flourishing variety of delightful woods, pleasant groves, lovely springs, together with spacious...rivers and creeks, it being a most healthful and pleasant situation." Alsop tried to convince indentured servants that they would like Maryland. He claimed that the servants already there "live well in the time of their service, and...they are made capable of living much better when they come to be free."

A typical Maryland planter of the mid-seventeenth century lived in a small, one-room house. With forests all around them, the planters cut down trees to build their homes. The wood was not aged, meaning it shrank or warped over time. Planters had to use clay or other soft materials to fill in the cracks that always appeared.

Most houses had wooden floors, but the poorest farmers walked on dirt inside their homes. The earliest homes in Maryland did not have glass windows. Planters either covered the window holes with oiled paper or left them open.

These simple wooden houses were cheap and easy to build. If a house needed repairs, a planter sometimes found it easier to abandon it and build a new one than to repair it. If planters did stay in one house, they usually added on rooms or built new buildings when they started families or hired servants.

Crops and Cash

Although tobacco was the main crop in Maryland, farms produced other goods as well. By law, the first settlers had to plant 2 acres (0.8 hectares) of corn for each acre of tobacco they raised. Lord Baltimore wanted to make sure the settlers did not starve. Most planters raised pigs, cattle, chickens, and their own fruits and vegetables. They bought some food, such as sugar and spices, and sometimes hunted wild game for meat.

In each county, a few planters usually emerged as the local merchants. They bought and sold goods that the settlers did not produce themselves. Some goods came from England and Virginia. Others came from traders who traveled through the Chesapeake region from the north.

Compared to families in northern colonies, Marylanders had a big advantage. They grew a crop they could easily sell overseas. The money the planters made from tobacco let them buy many of the goods they needed for daily life.

Some of the successful merchant-planters loaned money to other planters. The smaller planters often needed money if tobacco prices fell or corn crops failed. They could repay the loans when prices rose again. With hard work and some luck, a poor freeman could save enough money to rise up to the level of merchant-planter.

Manor Life

Maryland's farms were spread out along its many waterways. Most people lived far from each other, and Maryland did not develop major towns. Even St. Mary's City grew slowly. During the 1670s, one observer noted that the capital had only "30 houses spread five miles [8 kilometers] along the river's length and the buildings…[are] generally mean and little."

Although large plantations were rare, some planters built large homes called manor houses on their farms.

Large plantations were rare during Maryland's early years. Still, Lord Baltimore tried to create a kind of land ownership found in England. It was called the manor system. This made it possible for one planter to own several thousand acres. He would then sell or rent parcels of the land to freemen. The people who lived on the manors created their own communities. In some ways, they were independent of the social and economic life of the rest of the colony.

The owner of a manor was called the lord, though he probably had not actually received that title from the king. One of Maryland's lords was Thomas Gerrard. He owned thousands of acres near St. Clement Bay, on the southern end of the western shore of Chesapeake Bay. Gerrard raised all the common farm products of colonial Maryland. The most important were tobacco, corn, pigs, and cattle.

By 1660, the residents of Gerrard's manor were freemen who owned land, freemen who rented land, and indentured servants. Houses were scattered across St. Clement's Manor.

Freemen and indentured servants planted crops and worked the land for the lord of the manor.

If neighbors had a dispute, they settled the issues at the manor's own court, which served as the manor's government. It fined local Native Americans who stole from the settlers and shut down an illegal bar owned by a resident.

Manors such as Gerrard's did not last. Freemen who did not want to obey the lords moved farther inland, away from the bay. The manor lands also suffered from the constant growing of tobacco, which was so deadly to fertile soil. Freemen who did stay on the manor lands developed relations with people off the manor. These relationships became more important than their ties to the lord.

The Important Pig

To Marylanders, pigs provided much more than meat. Their hairs, called bristles, were used for brushes. Pigskin was turned into leather, and the animals' fat was used in cooking. Even pigs' blood could be used in a dish called blood pudding.

Trouble With the Puritans

Maryland's manors and plantations were far from England. Still, events in England often affected life in the colony. During the 1640s, several civil wars broke out in England. Some members of Parliament thought that King Charles I was a tyrant. They rebelled, seized control of the government, and killed Charles. The king's opponents included the Puritans. They had strict religious beliefs based on the Bible.

The Puritans opposed the Anglican Church, which was the established Protestant church in England.

Puritans had already come to America. They founded the Massachusetts Bay Colony in 1629. Some had also settled in Virginia and then moved into Maryland. The Puritans' rise to power in England led to political troubles in Maryland.

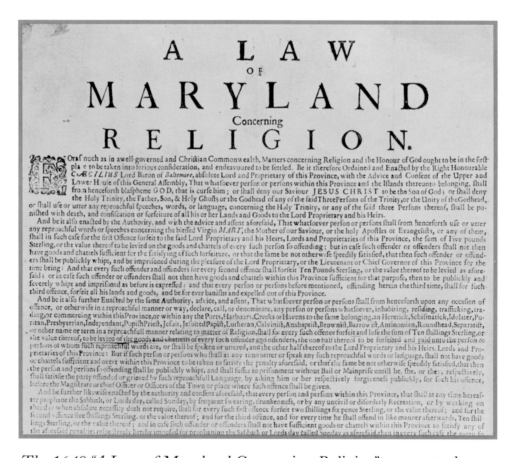

The 1649 "A Law of Maryland Concerning Religion" guaranteed religious freedom for all of Maryland's Christian residents.

In 1654, some Maryland Puritans accused the colony's leaders of rejecting Parliament's power. These Puritans worked with supporters in Virginia to take control of Maryland's government. They ended Lord Baltimore's proprietary rights. The Puritans also ignored the 1649 law granting religious freedom to all Christians. The Puritans said Roman Catholics could not freely practice their faith in Maryland. These actions led to a civil war in the colony.

The Puritans and Lord Baltimore's loyal supporters battled for control. Finally, in 1657, the Puritans accepted Lord Baltimore's claim to Maryland. This restored religious rights to Catholics and other groups in Maryland. Three years later, the Puritans in England allowed the son of Charles I to take power as King Charles II.

Maryland's Other Protestants

The Puritans were not the only notable group of Protestants in Maryland. The colony also had Quakers, Presbyterians, Anglicans, and members of smaller **sects**. Like Roman Catholics, Quakers could not freely practice their religion in England or in colonies controlled by the Puritans. In Massachusetts, several Quakers were killed because of their beliefs.

Since Maryland now accepted all Christian religions, the colony drew a small numbers of Quakers. They saw themselves as missionaries and eagerly sought new members. The Quakers believed that everyone had an "inner light" that brought them into direct contact with God. Believers did not need priests or ministers to help them understand the Bible or be good Christians.

The Quakers successfully converted some Maryland colonists to their religion. They built meetinghouses where they held their religious services. Many Quakers became successful merchants, and Quaker meetings sometimes turned into business events. One Quaker wrote that a meeting was "a kind of market…where the captains of ships and planters meet and settle their affairs."

Maryland's Presbyterians began arriving during the 1640s. They formed the first major group of Presbyterians in America. This religion developed in England and Scotland. In some ways, it was similar to Puritanism. In Maryland, the Presbyterians mostly lived on the Eastern Shore.

Anglicans were outnumbered by other religious groups in Maryland. In England, citizens had to pay taxes to support the Anglican Church. The Calverts did not collect taxes to pay for churches. But Maryland's Anglicans and other Protestants had to collect money to pay for ministers and build churches.

In 1676, one of the few Anglican ministers in the colony complained that the church needed more ministers to prevent the spread of sin. The minister wrote that "religion is despised, and all notorious vices are committed."

Over time, Maryland had more Protestants than Catholics. But through most of the seventeenth century, the Catholics could freely practice their faith. When the Puritans gave control back to Lord Baltimore, Maryland had restored the Catholics' rights. They enjoyed a religious freedom they could not find in England or in most of its other colonies.

Quakers often preached in the streets. They were the only religious group in the colonies that considered men and women equal.

The Decline of the Indians

The success of Lord Baltimore's colony slowly increased the European population in Maryland. By 1660, about 2,500 settlers lived there. That number continued to grow.

The arrival of the English led to major changes for Maryland's Algonquian Indians. The peaceful relations between Indians and settlers mostly lasted. But some colonists' actions upset the Algonquian. Settlers sometimes let their farm animals roam over Indian croplands. They also burned down Indian buildings to drive the Indians from their homes. These problems led to a few Indian attacks on the settlers. But usually the tribes retreated farther into the forest rather than confront the English.

The Indians also suffered from diseases the Europeans brought to North America. These included smallpox, measles, and the flu. The Native Americans had never been exposed to these diseases before. Their bodies did not have the natural defenses that would have helped them recover.

The Europeans also introduced the Indians to alcohol. The English traded hard liquor for furs. The result was that many Indians suffered from alcoholism. Drinking too much was often deadly for them.

During the 1650s, the settlers began setting aside land for the Native Americans on the western shore of the bay.

By the mid-1600s, the Algonquian way of life was quickly changing as more and more settlers drove the Indians from their traditional lands.

Later, the colonists created more of these reservations on the eastern side. On the reservations, the Indians were supposed to have the freedom to live as they wanted. But the settlers continued to press forward onto their lands.

Most Indians moved out of Maryland. They often settled with other tribes to the north and west. A few stayed and lived in English communities. Even the once mighty Susquehannock lost strength. Their numbers fell because of disease, war, and alcoholism. By the end of the seventeenth century, the settlers were the most powerful group of people in Maryland.

CHAPTER FOUR
Changing Times

The Growth of Slavery

By the end of the seventeenth century, Maryland's society began an important change. The servants who completed their indentures began their own farms. They wanted to buy their own servants to help them raise tobacco. At the same time, the wealthier planters needed more workers on their growing plantations. Planters of all classes could not find enough white Europeans to work as indentured servants. They increasingly turned to the slave markets to meet their needs.

The planters realized that slaves made economic sense. It was cheaper and easier to buy slaves than to hire new servants every few years. The slaves would never leave, as the servants did. The Chesapeake region of Maryland and Virginia was the first area in British North America to develop large plantations based on slave labor.

More and more Maryland tobacco farmers imported slaves to work their fields during the 1600s.

The shift from indentured servants to slaves began during the 1670s. As slavery grew, more laws were created in favor of slave owners. A 1671 law said that even if slaves became Christians, they had to remain slaves. At the same time, another law prevented slaves from entering into legal contracts. Over time, slaves were more likely to be executed for crimes, compared to freemen or servants. By the 1690s, planters had twice as many slaves as indentured servants.

Triangle Trade and the Middle Passage

The African slave trade of the seventeenth and eighteenth centuries united North America, Europe, and Africa. This formed the Triangle Trade. Ships made three stops on one round trip.

On one leg of the trip, ships might carry rum from England to Africa. The captains then picked up slaves and carried them to the West Indies or southern colonies in America. This was known as the Middle Passage. From there, the ships carried molasses or other goods back to England.

The Middle Passage was a horrible experience for the thousands of slaves who were forced to endure it. Hundreds of slaves were chained together below a ship's main deck. They received poor food and dirty water. Disease spread quickly on the voyage across the Atlantic Ocean. As many as 25 percent of the Africans died. Some of them committed suicide. They preferred death to the Middle Passage or the slavery waiting for them in America.

In the evening, slaves gathered together to socialize after the day's work was done. They often sang songs and told stories.

In 1697, Maryland had about 3,000 slaves. The colony's total population was less than 30,000. Less than fifteen years later, the colony had just under 8,000 slaves, out of a total population of about 46,000. Before and during this period, most slaves lived in the southern counties on both shores of the bay.

Most of the first African slaves arrived in Maryland from Virginia or the British West Indies. Some of these slaves had already learned a few words of English and received English names. White slave owners always renamed their slaves. With new names, the slaves lost connection to their old, free lives in Africa.

Slaves were captured in Africa, chained together, and marched to the African coast for sale. Those who could not keep up were left to die.

During most of the seventeenth century, many slaves in Maryland lived on small farms and worked side by side with their white masters and the indentured servants. In their free time, the slaves could grow vegetables in their own gardens or raise farm animals. The slaves often sold some of their crops or animals. By saving the money they made, some slaves were able to buy their freedom from their masters.

The New Slaves

As slavery became more common in Maryland, more of the slaves came directly from Africa. European slave traders set up bases along the West African coast, from Senegal to Angola. The Europeans worked with African slave traders. The Africans captured potential slaves, sometimes taking them from villages in the center of the continent. The captives were often separated from their families. Then the traders forced them to march in pairs while chained together at the ankles. Several pairs of slaves were tied together by ropes around their necks. The slaves might have to march this way for 300 miles (480 kilometers). Then they had to wait in crowded, jail-like cells until they were sold.

Colonial planters favored young men to work the fields, but women and children also served as slaves. They worked in their masters' homes, as well as on the farms. Most planters bought only a few slaves at a time, although wealthier planters might acquire several dozen.

Even then, Africans were often isolated from each other. Masters on large plantations often split their slaves into small groups. The masters then sent them to work and live on different parts of the plantation. This distance between groups made it hard for slaves to develop any sense of community. So did the number of languages the slaves spoke.

They often came from different parts of Africa and did not share a common language. Restrictions on the slaves' movements and the lack of women limited the growth of families. Most slaves led lonely lives.

Slave Life

For slaves, the few chances for social activities came on Sundays and in the evening. One Marylander described hearing slaves "beating their...drums by which they call considerable numbers of Negroes together in certain places." That freedom to move about and hold large gatherings ended as more slaves arrived in Maryland.

In the fields, slaves raised tobacco and corn and took care of pigs and cattle. On large plantations, they might also cut trees into lumber or press apples into cider. Other chores included chopping wood and clearing brush. Some slaves arrived from Africa with skills, such as carpentry, but masters preferred to use indentured servants in skilled positions. Slaves did the backbreaking work needed to run a plantation. Planters hired white men called overseers to make sure that the slaves did their jobs and did not run away.

The slaves lived in their own quarters, where they cooked their own meals. Slaves sent directly from Africa slept together in barracks. Most slaves born in America had their own small wooden shacks that they built themselves.

They slept on reeds or leaves covered with blankets, not real beds. The reeds and leaves sat on the shack's dirt floor.

Raising a family was hard for the slaves. Husbands and wives were sometimes separated and might even live on different plantations. Masters could overrule the parents' decisions about how to raise their children. They could also limit how much time slave husbands and wives spent with each other or their children.

Many slaves converted to Christianity and held their own religious services.

Political Changes

The rise of slavery came as Maryland went through major political changes. By the 1660s, Maryland's Assembly was split into two branches, or houses. The governor selected the upper house. Its members generally supported the interests of the Calverts and their friends in the colony. Voters elected the members of the lower house, who were called **delegates**. The lower house was called the House of Delegates. Its members tried to limit the power of the proprietor and his supporters.

In 1670, Governor Charles Calvert weakened the role of the freemen in the lower house. He placed limits on who could vote or run for political office, based on how much property they owned. Before this, all freemen could vote or hold office. A few years later, Calvert reduced the number of delegates each county elected from four to two. These changes, however, did not completely end the lower house's efforts to challenge the proprietor's rights.

A greater threat to the Calverts emerged in 1688. That year, events in England once again shaped Maryland's politics. Protestants in Parliament forced the Catholic king, James II, to leave the throne. Parliament replaced James with his daughter Mary, who was Protestant. Joining her as ruler was her husband William, a Dutch prince. After this so-called Glorious Revolution, Parliament had complete control over the English government. It also proclaimed that, in the future, every king or queen had to be Protestant.

The Glorious Revolution sparked Maryland's Protestants to seize control of the colony. They wanted to support William and Mary and end Catholic rule. The Protestants in Maryland outnumbered the Catholic forces that tried to defend the proprietor's rights.

The Protestants won their own revolution without any bloodshed. The Catholic governor left office, and in 1691, Queen Mary announced, "We have thought fit to take our province under our immediate care and protection." Maryland became a royal colony, and the Calverts no longer controlled it. From now on, the English crown would select the colony's governor.

The First School

Francis Nicholson saw the need for educated government workers. He used some of his own money to fund the colony's first free school, which opened in Annapolis in 1696. Tax money was used to keep the school running. Maryland's lawmakers waited several more decades before they funded schools in every county. Most children continued to be educated at home. Parents with money paid for their children to attend small private schools. The Annapolis free school eventually became St. John's College, which is still open today.

Protestants in Charge

Maryland's new government quickly made the Anglican Church the colony's established church. Now the church received tax funds to run its operations. Another change came in 1694. The capital was moved from St. Mary's City to a more central location, at Anne Arundel Town, named after the wife of the second Lord Baltimore. The new capital was renamed Annapolis. Governor Francis Nicholson helped plan the new capital. Annapolis soon featured the only brick church in Maryland and several inns for travelers.

The Old Trinity Church in Cambridge, Maryland, was founded in 1692. It is one of the oldest continuously operated churches in the country.

Maryland remained a royal colony until 1715, the year Charles Calvert died. Once again, a mixture of politics and religion led to a change in the colony's leadership. Calvert's son Benedict became the fourth Lord Baltimore. Benedict had converted to Protestantism. The new English king, George I, agreed to give Maryland back to the Calverts since the proprietor was not Catholic. George and future English rulers, however, kept the right to approve the colony's governors.

With this political change, Anglicanism remained the established church. Prejudice against Catholics also remained. During the early eighteenth century, the Assembly passed several laws that affected Catholics. They lost the freedom to worship in public or in private. They soon regained the right to worship in their homes, but prejudice against them remained strong. In 1718, the government took away the Catholics' right to vote or hold office. Maryland had been founded as a home for religious freedom. Now, its leaders trampled on the faith of the family who had founded it.

Colonial homes came in many shapes and sizes just as homes do today. The first colonists built their houses from materials they found in the New World. When ships from Europe arrived with supplies, the houses became sturdier and fancier.

❧ Many colonial houses had overlapping wooden siding called clapboards.

☙ The walls of the first colonial houses at Jamestown, Virginia, were made of sticks and mud called wattle and daub.

☞ The first settlers at Plymouth, Massachusetts, built shelters similar to Indian wigwams.

❧ The colonists planted gardens near their houses to grow fresh vegetables.

Houses

☞ In addition to houses, colonial farmers built windmills to provide power for sawmills and grain mills.

♨ Many of the first homes built by colonists were simple log cabins.

☞ Large houses like these were built in the 1700s.

⚱ Fences surrounded colonial gardens to keep out animals.

A MAP of
the most INHABITED part of
VIRGINIA
containing the whole PROVINCE of
MARYLAND
with Part of
PENSILVANIA, NEW JERSEY and NORTH CAROLINA
Drawn by
Joshua Fry & Peter Jefferson
in 1751.

Right Honourable, George Dunk Earl of Halifax First

st of the Right Honourable and Honourable Commissioners, for Tr

This Map is most humbly Inscribed to their Lords

By their Lordships

CHAPTER FIVE

Immigrants and Pioneers

Changes on the Farm

Through most of the seventeenth century, tobacco remained Maryland's top cash crop. But by the end of the century, the colony's economy began to change.

During the 1680s, the price of tobacco fell. Some farmers began to plant corn or other grains to sell, not just for their own use. Falling tobacco prices also forced some Marylanders to start their own businesses to raise money. In Somerset County, weavers from Scotland began to make and sell cloth. People were more likely to buy local products during tough economic times, since they were cheaper than goods from overseas.

☜ *Tobacco and other goods were shipped in and out of Baltimore's busy harbor during the 1700s. This drawing from 1751 was the cover of a map of the Virginia and Maryland colonies.*

Maryland craftsmen called coopers made the barrels used to store and ship tobacco and other goods.

More freemen turned to tenant farming to survive. They could not afford their own farms, so they rented land from wealthy planters. In the past, tenant farmers had been able to make enough money to eventually buy their own farms. This pattern changed in the eighteenth century. Most freemen who rented land now remained tenants for life. Since they did not own land, they could not vote, and so they could not take an active role in the colony's politics.

On Maryland's farms, large and small, more people began to make the items they needed. These goods included yarn and dairy products, and they were usually made by women. The colony's female population was rising. Part of this growth came from Maryland's natural increase. In other words, the number of births rose faster than the number of deaths. Slave families also saw this kind of natural increase, and the colony's overall population grew.

Starting in the 1680s, the servant population began to change. Young English residents were choosing to stay home or settle in other colonies. With tobacco prices low, Maryland no longer seemed to them a desirable place to live.

Many of the new servants were Irish. They came because they had few chances to find work in Ireland or other American colonies. Most English considered the Irish inferior. In the other colonies, masters would rather have English servants than Irish ones. But in Maryland, planters who needed workers took whomever they could find.

Still, the Irish faced prejudice in Maryland, partly because of their faith. Most Irish were Catholic. Some of the laws that were passed against Maryland's Catholics at the start of the early eighteenth century resulted from the arrival of the Irish.

Crafts and Industry

The changes in farm life led to the growth of some professions. To plant grains, farmers had to clear and plow fields. They could not just girdle trees as they had in the past. Planters needed more plows and other farm tools than they had before. This demand led to more work for artisans such as blacksmiths, woodworkers, and wheelwrights (wheel makers). When tobacco prices rose again, some skilled workers became planters. But some continued to practice their crafts while they farmed.

Apprentices

To give their sons a chance to learn skills, some parents signed contracts that made the boys apprentices for five or six years. As an apprentice, a boy lived with a skilled worker and learned his craft. The master was also supposed to teach the apprentice the basics of reading and writing. In return, the apprentice helped the master at his job. When the apprenticeship was over, the boy became a journeyman. He was free to go out on his own.

In Maryland, the government often set up orphans as apprentices. Under the law, orphans remained apprentices until they were twenty-one years old. Most of them trained with woodworkers, leatherworkers, and tailors. Some young girls also became apprentices. They learned such jobs as baking, weaving, and spinning. A girl might serve as an apprentice until she was eighteen or until she got married.

Large plantations sometimes had their own skilled workers, either indentured servants or slaves. Still, most relied on free craftsmen for their needs. Skilled servants cost more than unskilled laborers. Planters who could afford only a few servants were more likely to buy unskilled servants. Some planters taught themselves such skills as tailoring or woodworking so they would not have to pay for an artisan's services.

The colonies did not have industries that hired large numbers of workers. In general, England wanted the colonies to provide raw materials, such as lumber. The colonies then bought finished products made in England.

This system brought wealth to England, so the English government did not want the colonies to have their own industries. But by the eighteenth century, some colonies did have small mills and ironworks.

The Iron Industry

Maryland's first ironworks opened around 1715. Workers melted iron ore from local mines and shaped the liquid into bars. The iron bars were used to make tools and other products. Most of the iron bars were shipped to England after

Maryland's ironworks factories filled the air with smoke from the fires and furnaces used to melt and shape the iron.

1707. In 1719, the Maryland Assembly encouraged investors to open new ironworks. A planter who built an ironworks received 100 acres (41 hectares) of land. In addition, up to eighty workers would be excused from militia service and other public duties.

In response to the law, investors founded the Principio Iron Works in Cecil County. Like most ironworks, the company opened near a river. The water made it easy to bring in supplies and ship out finished products. A river's rushing water also turned waterwheels, which powered the plant's bellows. The bellows forced air into the furnace used to melt the iron ore.

In some ways, the Principio Iron Works was similar to a plantation. Both slaves and servants worked there. Some were taught how to do complex jobs. Workers grew some of their own food at the site. The company also ran a store that sold goods to employees and local residents. At its peak, Principio employed as many as 250 workers. They produced 20 tons (18 metric tons) of iron every week.

Important Investor

One of the owners of the Principio Iron Works was Augustine Washington, father of George Washington. When Augustine died, his share of the company went to his oldest son, Leonard. Money from the Maryland ironworks helped make the Washington family important members of Virginia's planter society.

The Rise of Baltimore

Grain farms and ironworks meant that Maryland was creating new jobs that were not related to tobacco. Another sign of the changing economy was the growth of a new city. Farmers and merchants on the northern end of the western shore of Chesapeake Bay needed their own port so they could ship goods to Great Britain. In 1729, a group of local residents bought land from a planter and founded Baltimore Town. Soon, the name was simply Baltimore.

Baltimore became a busy city and port in the 1700s, but farmers still grazed cattle at the edge of the town.

Maryland's Roads

The Great Wagon Road was nothing like today's wide, paved superhighways, or even local city streets. In colonial times, roads were usually old Indian trails that European settlers widened. New roads were built by county officials or private citizens. The Maryland Assembly passed laws to make sure that bridges on the roads were safe. But in 1724, the lawmakers noted that "the several bridges...are very much broken and out of repair, and several new bridges are still wanting." On Maryland's roads, travelers rode on horses or in horse-drawn carriages. Oxen often pulled carts carrying goods to market. Most people, however, did not travel long distances, so they walked wherever they had to go.

Baltimore sat along the Patapsco River. It had a deep port, so large ships could easily dock there. Rich farmlands surrounded the city, and the river could power grain mills, which turned raw grains into flour. Baltimore was also located near the Great Wagon Road, which linked Annapolis and Philadelphia, Pennsylvania. Using that road, farmers in western Maryland could reach Baltimore easier than they could get to Annapolis. Although the city's population grew slowly, Baltimore soon became an important trading center. It soon had an ironworks and became a leader in the milling business. Later in the eighteenth century, Baltimore was a center for shipbuilding in the Chesapeake region.

Into the Piedmont

Around the time Baltimore was founded, some settlers began moving farther away from Chesapeake Bay. They went into a region called the Piedmont. It lies just east of the Allegheny Mountains. Its name is French for "foot of the mountains."

The Piedmont stretches from Alabama to New York. In Maryland, the region separates the mountains from the low plains that border the Chesapeake. In the early eighteenth century, the Piedmont was an area of thick forests surrounded by hills. In Maryland, the Piedmont formed the edge of the western frontier. This land was far from the colony's main population.

Before European settlers came to the Piedmont, it was the home of several different Native American tribes. The first English colonists had limited contact with these tribes. Toward the end of the century, English traders in the Piedmont met the Shawnee. These Algonquian people had moved into the area from the southeast. From the north, the Susquehannock and other Iroquois had also settled in the region.

German immigrants who moved south from Pennsylvania were the first major group of European settlers in the Piedmont. The Germans usually belonged to small Protestant sects that had faced prejudice in their homeland. In Maryland's Piedmont, the Germans found excellent farmlands and religious freedom. Some Germans also went to Baltimore, where they entered its growing milling and shipping businesses.

Other new settlers in the region came from Ireland, though they were of Scottish descent. These "Scotch-Irish" were famous for their hard work as they settled remote regions of the frontier.

The Maryland Monster

During the 1730s, some problems arose in the Maryland Piedmont. The most important Marylander there was Thomas Cresap. He was a trader and land agent. He worked for a wealthy lawyer named Daniel Dulany. Cresap sold land in the Piedmont that Dulany owned. Cresap also bought and sold land himself, along the Susquehanna River and farther west.

Cresap's land near the river was close to the Pennsylvania border, and that colony's rulers claimed that the land belonged to them. In 1733, officials from Pennsylvania tried to arrest Cresap. He resisted, leading raids into Pennsylvania. People there soon called him "the Maryland Monster." He spent time in a Philadelphia jail, but in 1737, Maryland officials won his release.

Cresap continued to explore the Piedmont and bring new settlers to the region. Most bought land owned by Dulany. In 1745, Dulany realized that the area needed a town, so he founded Frederick Town, named for the sixth Lord Baltimore. It is now called simply Frederick. It became the largest city in the Piedmont. Frederick was also a stopping point for settlers moving westward. These pioneers eventually crossed the Piedmont and went over the Allegheny Mountains.

The Mason-Dixon Line

The squabble between Maryland and Pennsylvania over their shared border dated from the 1680s. The conflict continued after Thomas Cresap's problems in the region. In 1763, leaders from the two colonies finally agreed to hire outsiders to draw the boundary. Charles Mason and Jeremiah Dixon spaced stone markers 50 miles (80 kilometers) apart on the border. The new border they created became known as the Mason-Dixon Line. Later, the line was extended westward and marked the boundary between Pennsylvania and Virginia. The Mason-Dixon Line was also considered the boundary between the northern and southern states.

Frontier Life

The people who settled in the wilderness of the Piedmont had hard work ahead of them. Along Chesapeake Bay, the first settlers of Maryland had found some lands ready for farming. The region's Native Americans had already prepared the soil. But in the Piedmont, most Indians had stopped clearing out the forests. Disease and war had driven many of the tribes off their traditional lands. The settlers had to chop through overgrown bushes and trees to clear land for their homes and farms. Some settlers in the Piedmont built English-style houses, while others built log cabins or stone homes.

The settlers of the Piedmont grew little if any tobacco. The main crops were grains, especially corn. Some settlers also cut trees for lumber that they sold in the established communities along the coast. Many German immigrants raised cattle. The Germans built large, sturdy barns to house their cows and store their grain.

Slavery was rare in the Piedmont. Daniel Dulany sold the immigrants fairly small plots of land. The resulting farms were much smaller than the huge plantations that had developed along Chesapeake Bay. Farmers and their families could easily work these plots of lands with no outside help. Religion also played a role in limiting slavery in the

Piedmont. Some of the German Protestants who settled there believed that slavery was wrong.

The settlers' farms spread out around Frederick, while artisans and merchants lived in the town itself. Religious life was important for the German settlers. Frederick soon had churches serving several different sects. The settlers also attended the weekly markets. Dulany had started these "for buying and selling all sorts of cattle and other provisions of every kind." After 1748, Frederick was also the seat of the county's government.

Danger at Sea

During the late seventeenth century, residents on Chesapeake Bay faced the threat of pirates. Most pirates sailed farther south in the Atlantic Ocean, but a few did reach the upper portions of the bay. Governor Francis Nicholson asked the English government to send naval ships to protect Maryland's merchant ships, and a few pirates were caught in Maryland's waters. One legend in Talbot County says that local residents made a deal with one pirate. They gave him land in the county and he agreed to end his piracy.

CHAPTER SIX

Success and Troubles

Maryland's "Golden Age"

The middle decades of the eighteenth century have sometimes been called Maryland's Golden Age. Its economy was strong, and Maryland's elite citizens had riches the first settlers could not have imagined. Even planters with medium and small farms could afford to spend more on everyday items. They bought silverware, fancy dishes, clothing, and books.

Most of the wealthiest planters now focused on running their farms. On the whole, the planters did not want to risk their wealth in business ventures. A separate class of merchants arose to handle the buying and selling of goods. These businessmen replaced the merchant-planters of the seventeenth century.

🐚 *Maryland's wealthy planters enjoyed many luxuries, including smoking the tobacco they grew on their plantations.*

Maryland's wealthy planters controlled politics and the economy. They **dominated** the lower house of the Assembly and tried to weaken the power of the proprietor. The freemen who rented land or ran their own small farms largely accepted the planters' control. Most Marylanders continued to believe that some people were naturally more suited to govern than others.

Fancy dances called balls were one way that Maryland plantation owners enjoyed their wealth.

The wealthy planters had great influence in the Assembly, so they could direct its actions. Still, at times small planters and artisans challenged the political views of the wealthy. They sometimes voted planters who ignored their interests out of office. Maryland's proprietors could overturn laws passed in the Assembly. But on the whole, they did not use that power often during the eighteenth century.

Maryland's political **elite** had local powers most American colonists lacked. Under Maryland's charter, the laws passed in the colony could not be reviewed by the British government. By the eighteenth century, only Maryland, Rhode Island, and Connecticut enjoyed that right.

Golden Lifestyle

By the mid-eighteenth century, most wealthy planters had been born and raised in the colony. They modeled their lives on the "gentlemen" who dominated British society. The planters wanted to be accepted as equals with the elite of Great Britain. The British elite, however, usually looked down on the successful colonists. The colonists' wealth and local power did not compare to the riches and power that the British elite enjoyed.

Marylanders who were not accepted among the British elite tried to show off their importance within the colony. Some built huge brick mansions, with finely detailed craftwork inside. A planter who served in the government might also have a townhouse in Annapolis. The planters and professional men, especially lawyers, often met at social clubs, where they ate, drank, and talked. The clubs gave the members a chance to have fun without any concern for their daily affairs. One club did not allow its members to discuss politics.

In their homes, the planters treated guests to fine meals and entertainment. A breakfast might include beef, ham, and deer meat, along with coffee and breads. Some mansions had ballrooms where their owners held dances. The planters hired musicians to play for their guests. Indentured servants or slaves with musical skills also played for their masters.

The Sport of Kings

English aristocrats had enjoyed horseracing for centuries. Maryland's elite shared their passion for raising and racing horses. During the eighteenth century, Annapolis became the center of horseracing in the Chesapeake region. The races usually featured other popular activities, such as gambling and drinking. The mixture of alcohol and strong feelings about the races led to frequent fistfights. The fights became another attraction at the races.

In other rooms, the partygoers chatted and played cards. William Eddis, a British official sent to Annapolis in 1769, noted that all Americans were good hosts. But one Maryland planter, he wrote, "has established a **preeminence** which places his character in an exalted point of view."

The Other Side of the Golden Age

Not everyone enjoyed the luxury found on Maryland's largest plantations. Many free whites still could not afford to buy their own land. And the wealth of the powerful planters came mostly from the hard work of slaves.

Maryland's planters did not buy as many slaves as the planters in the Carolinas or Virginia did. Through the mid-eighteenth century, the Marylanders also employed servants, convicts, and freemen. But slavery continued to grow. Many of the slaves were now born and raised on Maryland's plantations, and the elite owned most of them.

During his stay in Maryland, William Eddis found that slaves there were "better fed, and better treated, than their unfortunate brethren...in our West India islands." Still, slaves were considered property, not free people, and masters often treated them harshly. The law rarely punished a master who mistreated slaves. On the other hand, the court system punished blacks more severely than it did whites. Slaves who stole, for example, were usually hanged.

Out of Slavery

By the middle of the eighteenth century, almost all black Americans in Maryland were slaves. Still, the colony had a number of free blacks, more than other British colonies. Some were the children and grandchildren of servants or slaves who had won their freedom in the seventeenth century. Most were mulattoes. Some planters gave mixed-blood slaves their freedom when they were too old to do heavy labor. But even when they were free, black Americans had to worry about laws that might force them back into slavery.

One well-known freed slave family was the Bannekays, better known today as the Bannekers. Mary Bannekay was the free daughter of an African slave and an English indentured servant. She freed a slave on her farm and married him. Their children included a son named Benjamin. Benjamin Banneker became the most famous free black American in eighteenth-century Maryland. He was a skilled mathematician and engineer. During the 1790s, he helped design the nation's new capital city of Washington, D.C.

In 1739, a group of slaves in Prince George's County planned to revolt against their masters. The masters learned about the plan and punished the leaders. Local residents also set up guards around public buildings in Annapolis. Maryland's leaders discussed their fear of "being sacrificed to the rage and fury of merciless and barbarous slaves." They seemed to ignore that slavery itself created the slaves' anger.

Threats in the West

In 1754, troops led by George Washington traveled deep into Virginia's western territory. France also claimed this land and built a fort at what is now Pittsburgh, Pennsylvania. Washington's mission was to drive the French out of the region. His men battled a small group of French troops, killing ten of them. This battle marked the start of the French and Indian War. In this conflict, British and American forces battled with the French and their Indian allies for control of North America.

Washington's attack led to a much larger French attack on the Virginians. The French beat them badly. Washington and his troops retreated into western Maryland, where they built Fort Cumberland. In Annapolis, the Assembly realized that Maryland was threatened by this conflict. The lawmakers ordered Thomas Cresap to organize a militia and defend the colony's western borders.

In 1755, British troops landed in Virginia. Militias from Virginia and Maryland joined this force. They marched from Fort Cumberland to fight the French and their Indian allies in Pennsylvania. The British lost. Maryland governor Horatio Sharpe said, "It is as surprising a defeat, I think, as has been heard of." With the British defeat, the French and

Indians still posed a threat to the colonial frontier. In Maryland, some families moved east for safety.

To help pay for the war effort, the Maryland Assembly approved new taxes in 1756. As in the past, the lawmakers tried to assert their authority over the Calverts. Ignoring orders from Governor Sharpe, they taxed the proprietors' lands. The tax law gave the lower house more control over the colony's military and economic affairs. The Calverts accepted the taxes only out of loyalty to Britain's King George II. They did not want the king to think that they were unwilling to help defend British North America.

The colony resisted new calls for help in fighting the war. The colonists considered themselves loyal British subjects. Yet they were also used to controlling their own affairs. That desire for independence would rise again in the years to come.

Peace and New Problems

In the late 1750s, Great Britain won several major battles in Canada, ending the French and Indian War. In 1763, France and Great Britain signed a peace treaty that gave Great Britain control of France's territories in North America.

Western Maryland, however, still faced the threat of violence. Native Americans who had supported the French began attacking British forts along the frontier. An Ottawa

Acadians in Maryland

As the French and Indian War began, Great Britain controlled Nova Scotia, Canada. This colony had many citizens of French descent, known as Acadians. The British forced the Acadians to leave Nova Scotia. Five boat-loads of them landed in Maryland.

Maryland's Protestant rulers disliked the Acadians because they were both French and Roman Catholic. The government prevented Maryland's Catholics from offering the Acadians much aid. During the late 1760s, most of the Acadians in Maryland joined a larger Acadian settlement in Louisiana. That region became the home of a large French-speaking community. Today, the Acadians there are known as Cajuns.

The Acadians were descended from French trappers. They brought their traditions and language to Maryland.

Indian named Pontiac led this rebellion. He and other tribal leaders feared that more English immigrants would now swarm over Indian lands. Already, the tribes and the settlers sometimes battled each other on those lands.

The British fought Pontiac and his forces for several years before ending the Indian threat. By now, George III was king of Great Britain. To keep the Americans away from the Indians, he ordered the American colonists not to move westward across the Allegheny Mountains. The British also planned to station more troops along the frontier in order to prevent future violence between colonists and Native Americans.

British officials wanted the Americans to help pay for the troops on the western frontier and for the costs of the French and Indian War. Britain also wanted to remind the colonists that Parliament and the king ruled them. They were not as independent as they wanted to be.

In 1764, Parliament passed the Sugar Act. This law placed special taxes, called duties, on certain items brought into the colonies. The taxed items included sugar, molasses, coffee, and lumber. The Sugar Act also called for strict penalties against colonists who tried to **smuggle** goods into America. One of the favorite smuggled items was molasses, the main ingredient in rum.

In 1765, another British attempt to tax the colonists created a stir in Maryland. Parliament passed the Stamp Act. This law forced the colonists to pay a tax when they used paper documents of all kinds. The colonists then received a stamp that they placed on the document to prove they had paid the tax. The Stamp Act applied to legal papers, business documents, newspapers, and college degrees. Even playing cards were taxed.

Since so many items were taxed, the Stamp Act affected a wide range of Marylanders, including such important people as merchants, ministers, lawyers, and publishers. In Maryland, and across the colonies, many Americans prepared to fight the new tax.

Newspapers in Maryland

Many Marylanders first heard about the Stamp Act in the pages of the *Maryland Gazette*. Founded in 1727, this newspaper was printed in Annapolis. The weekly *Gazette* was Maryland's first newspaper. Like most colonial papers, the *Gazette* published business and political news. It also featured letters from Europe and articles by local writers.

The Stamp Act required colonists to pay for a stamp such as this before they could buy paper products.

CHAPTER SEVEN

Revolutionary Maryland

Tax Troubles

The Stamp Act came at a bad time for many Marylanders. Tobacco prices had fallen, and all trade was down. One Calvert family member wrote to a relative, "Our trade is ruined, we are immensely in debt, and not the least probability of getting ourselves clear. Our [jails] are not half large enough to hold the debtors." Paying a new tax at this time seemed impossible to some people. But people who did not pay their taxes or owed debts could be thrown in jail.

Foes of the Stamp Act claimed that the tax violated British law. British citizens, through their elected representatives, had to approve taxes that directly affected them. But

Colonists reacted to the Stamp Act with marches and demonstrations. They carried signs criticizing the British government for taxing the colonies.

the colonists were not represented in Parliament. This meant they had had no chance to oppose the Stamp Act or shape its language. The new law was an example of "taxation without representation." The colonists would not stand for it.

Against the Stamp Act

Across the colonies, people protested the Stamp Act. They wanted Parliament to **repeal**, or end, the law. The protesters became known as Patriots. Colonists who accepted British policies were called Tories or Loyalists.

Some Patriots formed groups called the Sons of Liberty, which organized the protests. They and their supporters met in public squares and commons. They gathered at certain trees that were soon called Liberty Trees. Maryland's first Sons of Liberty group was formed in November 1765. By then, many Marylanders had already shown their disgust with the Stamp Act.

In August 1765, British officials chose Zacharias Hood of Annapolis to collect the tax and give out the stamps. An angry mob created a life-sized doll that looked like Hood and burned it. Later, a crowd burned down a warehouse that Hood had rented to store the stamps.

Marylanders also protested with words. Daniel Dulany the Younger was a lawyer like his successful father. He wrote a pamphlet attacking the Stamp Act and Parliament's right to tax the colonies at all. "The colonies claim the privileges of British subjects," Dulany wrote. "It has proved to be inconsistent with those privileges to tax them without their **consent**." Dulany's pamphlet was read across the colonies and in London.

Along with their protests, Americans pledged to stop buying British goods until Parliament repealed the Stamp Act. British merchants knew they would lose money because of this **boycott**. They pressured the British government to repeal the tax. Parliament agreed, but at the same time, it claimed the right to tax the colonies in the future.

Parliament took that step in 1767. It passed a new round of duties on certain goods such as paints, paper, and tea. The Townshend Acts also tried once again to end smuggling in the colonies. By now, however, Maryland's economy had improved. Not many Marylanders spoke out against the Townshend Acts.

Still, merchants in the Northeast called for another boycott of British goods. In 1769, Baltimore's merchants decided to join them. In Annapolis, an association of

The Stamp Act Congress

During the Stamp Act protests, political leaders in Massachusetts wanted to meet with other colonial lawmakers. The Massachusetts leaders thought that the colonies should work together during the crisis. Delegates from Maryland and eight other colonies met in New York City for the Stamp Act Congress. The congress marked the first time that the colonies united to oppose British policies.

"merchants, traders, freeholders, mechanics, and other inhabitants" of the capital region also took part. They declared that the Townshend Acts "deprive us in the end of all political freedom."

The Calm Before the Storm

Once again, American boycotts had an effect. In 1770, Parliament repealed the duties, except for the one on tea. Some colonies refused to import the tea, but Maryland's merchants began buying it again. Life was returning to normal in Maryland, and for the next three years the colony was calm. One resident noted in a letter to England, "Politics are scarce talked of."

Maryland's Tea Party

In October 1774, Marylanders staged their own protest against British tea. The *Peggy Stewart* arrived in Annapolis carrying 20,000 tons (18,000 metric tons) of tea. The ship's owner, Anthony Stewart, upset local Patriots when he paid the duty on the tea. Fearing for his life, Stewart admitted that he had "committed a most daring insult" by ordering the tea. The Patriots were still not happy, so Stewart agreed to burn the tea and the *Peggy Stewart*. With the ship aflame, the Patriots were satisfied.

Coffins with the initials of four of the men killed in the Boston Massacre appeared in this drawing, which was printed in newspapers throughout the colonies.

In Massachusetts, however, trouble continued to brew. In March 1770, British troops stationed in Boston killed five Americans. For many months, Patriot leaders condemned this "Boston Massacre."

Three years later, the city's Patriots protested a new law, the Tea Act. The act lowered the price on tea sold by the British East India Company but kept the taxes on tea sold by local merchants. This was seen by colonists as an attempt by the British government to control the sale of this popular product in America. More importantly, colonists saw it as an attempt to control their lives.

The Boston Tea Party

Late at night on December 16, a group of men dressed as Indians raided three ships docked in Boston Harbor. The ships were loaded with tea. Working silently, the raiders threw hundreds of chests of tea into the water to protest the Tea Act.

News of this "Boston Tea Party" quickly spread to the other colonies. William Eddis was still working in Annapolis at this time. In May 1774, he wrote, "All America is aflame!… The colonists are ripe for any measure that will tend to the preservation of what they call their natural liberty."

After the Boston Tea Party, the British punished Massachusetts. Parliament passed a series of laws that limited

Sons of Liberty dumped bales of tea into Boston Harbor, sparking protests against the British throughout the colonies.

the powers of local government and put the colony under military rule. The new laws closed Boston Harbor and stopped goods, including food, from entering the city. Businesses closed; people lost their jobs and ran short of food. In the colonies these laws were called the Intolerable Acts, and they stirred sympathy for Massachusetts across America.

The colonies decided to meet to discuss how to respond to the Intolerable Acts. In September 1774, delegates from every colony except Georgia met in Philadelphia at the First Continental Congress. The delegates debated for several weeks. Some argued that the colonies should go to war with Great Britain. Others wanted to avoid violence. In the end, the First Continental Congress agreed that the colonists could not be deprived of their "life, liberty, or property" without their consent.

In Massachusetts, Patriots prepared to fight the British soldiers stationed there. The local militias trained and gathered guns and supplies. On April 18, 1775, British troops began marching out of Boston to the nearby Massachusetts town of Concord. Their mission was to capture military supplies that the colonists had stored there. The next morning, in both Lexington and Concord, British soldiers and colonial militia clashed for the first time. When the fighting was over, more than 250 British troops were dead or wounded. Fewer than 100 Patriots were killed. The Revolutionary War had begun.

A Time of Change

During the unrest caused by British taxes, the colonists in Maryland were not as affected as those in larger colonies. As time passed, however, the protests spilled over into Maryland, causing a change in the colonial government.

Maryland at this time was still mostly rural. Baltimore was now Maryland's commercial center. It was also the largest city, with a population of 6,000. Yet Baltimore was small compared to other major American cities. Boston and Philadelphia were three times as big.

The Potomac River valley was typical of Maryland's rural countryside in the eighteenth century.

The colony's entire population was about 220,000. This placed it in the middle of the thirteen colonies, in terms of population. Black Americans made up about one-third of that total, one of the highest percentages in America. Almost all of them were slaves.

Maryland's great planters and wealthy merchants still controlled society. They were also the main Patriot leaders in the colony. For the most part, the Patriots also opposed the proprietors and their representatives in the colony.

In June 1774, the Maryland Patriots held a new political meeting. They called it the provincial convention. Counties elected representatives, who discussed colonial events and British policies. A second convention met in November. The governor chosen by the proprietor soon realized that he could not control the Patriots. The provincial convention began to act as Maryland's unofficial government.

Declaring Independence

Just after the fighting at Lexington and Concord, the Second Continental Congress met in Philadelphia. The delegates soon chose George Washington to serve as the commander of the new Continental army. But most delegates still hoped that the British and Americans could avoid a total war. Only a few delegates suggested declaring independence from Great Britain.

Fighting continued between the colonists and British troops through 1775. More members of the Second Continental Congress came to think that the colonies should declare their independence.

They decided to appeal to the king one last time. The Continental Congress sent a letter to King George III asking him to settle the differences between England and the colonies peacefully. The king refused and declared that his army should "bring the traitors to justice." The colonists knew they had no choice except to declare their independence from British rule.

They called upon Thomas Jefferson from Virginia to write a document declaring that the colonies now considered themselves free and independent. Jefferson was known for

Maryland's Signers for Independence

These delegates to the Second Continental Congress signed the U.S. Declaration of Independence.

Samuel Chase was one of the first judges to sit on the U.S. Supreme Court.

William Paca held many government positions and served as governor after the war.

Thomas Stone was asked to serve as a delegate to the Constitutional Convention of 1787. He declined because of his wife's poor health.

Charles Carroll of Carrollton helped write Maryland's first state constitution and later served as a U.S. senator.

his powerful writing ability. The document that he produced was called the Declaration of Independence. It became one of the most important documents in American history.

Jefferson presented his declaration to the Congress on June 28, 1776. After discussions and revisions, Congress voted to accept the document on July 4 and signed it about one month later. This marked the moment when the colonies became the United States of America.

Maryland now no longer was an English colony but one of the thirteen states of the United States of America. Maryland's lawmakers soon wrote the state's first constitution, creating a new state government. The Assembly still had two houses. Voters elected the members of the lower house. They chose special electors who chose senators, the members of the upper house. The lawmakers then elected the governor.

The constitution also had a bill of rights. These rights included freedom of the press and the right to a trial by jury. Still, not everyone was allowed to vote. The constitution said that only free males who owned property could elect representatives to the new Assembly.

Maryland at War

Not all Marylanders or all Americans wanted independence from Great Britain. At the start of the Revolutionary War, America had a population of about 2.2 million. Historians think that about one-third of those people actively supported independence. Another third were Tories. The rest were neutral or supported whoever seemed to be winning at a particular time. Marylanders also split in their support for the war, but the exact number of Patriots and Tories is unknown.

As early as December 1774, some Marylanders prepared for war with Great Britain. Frederick Town formed a militia and began training. Later, General George Washington wanted a force in Maryland and nearby states that could quickly move into battle. Many troops joined this force, which was called the Flying Camp Battalion.

Maryland escaped British invasion during the Revolutionary War. British troops landed in the state in 1777, but they marched into Delaware on their way to Philadelphia. Still, Marylanders played a major role at some key battles.

In August 1776, Marylanders fought in Washington's Continental army in New York. They showed their bravery at the Battle of Long Island. Just 400 Maryland soldiers held off 10,000 British troops. As the Marylanders attacked, thousands of other American soldiers safely retreated through a swamp. On a hill, General Washington watched the British killing the Marylanders. "Good God," he said, "what brave fellows I must this day lose!" Overall, the Battle of Long Island was a terrible loss for the Americans. Still, Maryland's troops had saved most of Washington's army.

Painter of the Revolution

Another famous Marylander who fought in the Revolution was Charles Willson Peale. As a teenager, he worked as an apprentice to a saddle maker. He later taught himself how to paint and studied art in England.

When the war started, Peale joined the Pennsylvania militia. He fought in several battles, but he also found time for his art. He painted battle scenes and fellow soldiers. He also painted the first official portrait of George Washington.

After the war, Peale continued to paint the portraits of America's leaders. He is sometimes called the Painter of the Revolution. Peale had two sons who were also painters. In 1813, one of them opened Maryland's first art museum.

Charles Willson Peale

German immigrants from western Maryland had their own regiment. They fought for the Continental army at important battles in New Jersey and Pennsylvania. They also spent the winter of 1777 at Valley Forge, Pennsylvania. At this camp, thousands of soldiers died from disease and starvation.

One of Maryland's great heroes during the Revolutionary War was John Eager Howard. He showed his bravery and skill at several key battles in the Carolinas. He was one of just eight soldiers to receive a medal from Congress for his service. U.S. general Henry "Light-Horse Harry" Lee wrote that Howard was "always to be found where the battle raged."

Some Marylanders helped fight the war without ever picking up guns. On some plantations, women took over jobs once done by men. The women raised food for both soldiers and civilians. The state's women also gathered blankets and clothes and sent them to the troops.

Maryland doctor James Craik also played a key role during the Revolutionary War. Washington named him the army's top doctor. Craik set up hospitals for wounded soldiers and sometimes took care of them himself.

Black Americans During the War

Maryland's black Americans also fought for their country's independence. At first, the white leaders in most states did not want to arm blacks, either slave or free. Whites had always feared that black with guns might use them to rebel. But as the war went on, the states needed more soldiers.

By 1780, a number of free blacks and mulattoes had joined Maryland's militia. In some cases, blacks served in place of whites who did not want to fight. They also served as ships' pilots and guided boats through Chesapeake Bay.

Slaves also played a part in the war. The British promised to free any slaves who joined their side. Thousands of slaves escaped from southern plantations to fight for the British. Early in the war, Maryland sent troops to St. Mary's City to prevent local slaves from joining the British troops. Still, hundreds of Maryland's slaves managed to escape from their masters and fight for Great Britain.

The Maryland Line

Many of the recruits from Maryland formed what was called the Maryland Line. This was a Patriot military unit made up of men from Maryland. By some reports, George Washington referred to these troops as the Old Line. Today, one of Maryland's nicknames is the Old Line State.

As the need for troops rose, Maryland decided to use its own slave soldiers. In October 1780, the Assembly allowed slaves to volunteer. One Maryland general wrote, "I am of the opinion that the Blacks will make excellent soldiers."

Most black American soldiers remained privates. Many worked as servants for American officers or cooked for the other men. Other blacks were drummers. At the time, soldiers on both sides entered battle to the beat of a drum.

Peter Salem was one of the most famous black American soldiers who fought for the Patriots. He shot Britain's Major Pitcairn at the battle of Lexington in Massachusetts.

Slaves received their freedom for fighting, if they survived the war. Army life was often easier than living on plantations. For their service, free blacks received money or land. They might not have been able to earn these rewards any other way.

At War's End

In October 1781, the Americans defeated the British at Yorktown, Virginia. This major loss led Parliament to halt the war. The British agreed to grant the United States its independence. Some fighting continued, but for most Americans the war was over. Great Britain and the United States signed a peace treaty in November 1782, and the Continental Congress approved it the next year.

When the fighting ended, the congress was still meeting in Philadelphia. But at the end of 1783, the lawmakers briefly met at the State House in Annapolis. On December 23, George Washington resigned as general there. A few weeks later, the congress gave final approval to the peace treaty with Great Britain. The war was officially over. Now Maryland and the other states had to govern themselves as an independent nation.

THE COLONIAL GAZETTE.

Num. 39.]   SUPPLEMENT.   Price

Oct.   1781

LETTER FROM GEN. WASHINGTON TO THE GOVERNOR OF MARYLAND, ANNOUNCING THE S
OF CORNWALLIS.

CAMP NEAR YORK, OCT.,

DEAR SIR : Inclosed I have the honor of transmitting to your Excellency the terms upon which L
wallis has surrendered the Garrisons of York and Gloucester.

We have not been able yet to get an account of prisoners, ordnance or stores in the different dep
but from the best general report there will be (officers included) upwards of seven thousand men, beside
more than 70 pieces of brass ordnance and a hundred of iron, their stores and other valuable articles.

My present engagements will not allow me to add more than my congratulations on this happy eve
express the high sense I have of the powerful aid which I have derived from the State of Maryland in
with my every request to the execution of it. The prisoners will be divided between Winchester, in Vir
Fort Frederick, in Maryland. With every sentiment of the most perfect esteem and regard, I have the ho

Your Excellency's most obedient and humble servant,   G. WASHIN

The French at Yorktown.

Few things, indeed, suggested by the history of the war are more instructive than a parallel between the fate of Burgoyne and the fate of Cornwallis. The defeat of Washington on Long Island and the loss of New York had been attributed to the fact that his troops

carrying 1,700 guns, and 19,000 seamen. On the la
Rochambeau with French troops, aggregating 8,400 men
Continental troops under Washington, together with 3,
who were of less account. Against this military and

CHAPTER EIGHT

Building a New Government

Problems Across the Country

During the Revolutionary War, the Continental Congress had passed the Articles of Confederation. The articles created the first national government for the United States. The individual states kept most powers. The congress's main job was to run the war effort and deal with foreign nations. It could not collect taxes or control trade among the states. The new government lacked the power to force the states to accept the laws it passed.

After the war, the United States faced many problems. The British refused to pull out all their troops in the west. The Americans also argued with Spain. At the time, Spain

✎ *The* Colonial Gazette *from October 1781 features a letter from General George Washington to the governor of Maryland, announcing the surrender of Cornwallis at Yorktown.*

controlled New Orleans, the port at the mouth of the Mississippi River. The Spanish wanted to restrict the Americans' use of the river. The congress also owed money to foreign countries. It had borrowed these funds to pay for the war. The states also had their own debts. They were not always willing to give the congress what they had promised to pay.

The Continental Congress met in Maryland's Old Senate Chamber in Annapolis in 1783.

Many U.S. political leaders believed that the country needed a stronger central government. They wanted to create a federal system. Under this system, the country would balance powers more evenly between the states and the national government. States would still pass their own laws and control the local governments. But they would give up some of their powers to the federal, or national, government.

In September 1786, representatives from five states met in Annapolis. They discussed the need for a new, stronger government. They called on all the states to meet at a convention the next May in Philadelphia. Today, this meeting is called the Constitutional Convention. Every state except Rhode Island sent delegates to the convention.

Writing the Constitution

The Constitutional Convention lasted for more than three months. The delegates held different views on what kind of government to create. Some argued that the new government had to have more power than the congress did under the Articles of Confederation. Others wanted to limit the new government's powers as much as possible. A few delegates even argued that the convention did not have the power to create a new government. All it could do was try to improve the Articles of Confederation.

The states tended to fall into two groups. The states with small populations feared giving the larger states too much power in the new government. Maryland usually sided with the small states.

James McHenry of Baltimore worried about a plan to let a new congress control trade between the states. He believed that the largest states would end up dominating trade. McHenry wrote, "We almost shuddered at the fate of the commerce of Maryland, should we be unable to make a change to this extraordinary power." In the end, the delegates gave Congress the power to control trade between the states.

Maryland sent a total of five delegates to the Constitutional Convention. Not all of them attended at the same time. And they did not always agree on certain issues. In the end, two of Maryland's five delegates did not sign the Constitution. One of them was Luther Martin. He had opposed creating a new government at all. He had wanted to improve the Articles of Confederation.

Martin and other Americans who opposed the Constitution believed

The First President

The states ratified, or approved, the Articles of Confederation in March 1781. The Second Continental Congress was now called the Congress of the Confederation. The new congress chose Maryland's John Hanson as its first president. Unlike today's presidents, Hanson had few powers. His main job was to run the congress's daily affairs. Hanson served as president until November 1782.

that the new government took too much power away from the states. They also feared that the federal government would restrict personal freedoms. Martin wanted a bill of rights, like the one in Maryland's state constitution. He later wrote that the new federal Constitution would be "injurious to my country."

The delegates to the Constitutional Convention debated the new constitution for months before signing it.

The Slavery Issue

One difficult issue the delegates debated was slavery. Some northern states had already begun to end slavery. But southern states, such as Maryland, believed that their economy would collapse without it. The southern delegates said that they would reject the Constitution if the northern states tried to end slavery everywhere. Instead, the delegates gave each state the power to decide on its own what to do about slavery.

Many of the nation's most important leaders, including George Washington, were slave owners .

Slavery was also a concern for political reasons. The new Congress was to consist of two houses. The Senate would have two senators from each state. In the House of Representatives, the number of representatives from each state would be based on its population. The question was whether to count slaves as part of a state's population. If slaves were counted, southern states with many slaves would have more representatives in the House of Representatives than they would otherwise. Southern states would also pay more in taxes if slaves were counted, because the new federal taxes were going to be based on population.

The southern delegates wanted to count slaves when deciding how many representatives a state would have. But they did not want to count slaves for taxes. The convention decided on a compromise. Every five slaves would count as three persons in a state's population. They would be counted this way both for deciding on the number of representatives and for paying taxes. In return, southern states agreed that the United States would end its slave trade with foreign countries in 1808. This Three-Fifths Compromise helped win support for the Constitution.

Although the delegates talked about slavery, the words *slaves* and *slavery* were not mentioned in the Constitution. The new government also ignored the legal rights of free blacks. Maryland and other states would continue to deny them their rights until after the Civil War ended in 1865.

Maryland and the New Constitution

The states had to ratify the Constitution before it could take effect. In April 1788, delegates from across Maryland met to debate the Constitution. Some of them repeated Luther Martin's call for a bill of rights. Most delegates, however, accepted the Constitution as it was written. Maryland was the seventh state to **ratify** the new government. A few months later, the Constitution took effect. The new Congress met for the first time in April 1789. That same month, George Washington became the first president elected under the Constitution.

However, the idea of a bill of rights had not gone away. Congress passed ten amendments, or changes, for the states to approve. They dealt with protecting personal freedoms. These included free speech, freedom of religion, and freedom of the press. These amendments were called the Bill of Rights. Maryland ratified them in December 1789.

Federal Hill

On May 1, 1788, large crowds filled the streets of Baltimore to celebrate the approval of the Constitution. The festival also included a parade. The area where the people celebrated is now known as Federal Hill.

Entering a New Era

In 1790, the U.S. government took its first census, or count of the population. Maryland had roughly 209,000 whites and 103,000 slaves. Its population also included about 8,000 free blacks.

The state's economy was doing well. Slaves, however, did not benefit from that wealth. Their lack of freedom paid for the gains of Maryland's planters. Yet not all success in Maryland rested on slavery. Western farmers continued to grow crops on their own. New businesses appeared in Baltimore. Its population had doubled since the start of the war, and the city's ships carried goods around the world.

Maryland would also benefit from the building of Washington, D.C. The nation's new capital city rose along the Potomac River on land that had once been part of Maryland and Virginia. In years to come, the national government would locate some of its offices in Maryland.

In a few decades, Maryland had gone from being the private lands of one family to an independent state. Then the Constitution defined its role as one of the states in a new country, the United States of America. Many changes and challenges still lay ahead.

Recipe
Crab Stew

Early colonists in Maryland found a good supply of food in Chesapeake Bay. The bay was filled with fish and shellfish. Some settlers claimed they found crabs so large that one crab could feed four hungry men. Even today, Maryland is famous for its crabs.

Here is a traditional recipe for crab stew.

1 medium onion
1 medium tomato
4 sprigs fresh parsley or
1 teaspoon dried parsley
1/4 cup butter
1 pound crabmeat
(fresh, frozen, or canned)
1/2 teaspoon salt
1/2 teaspoon nutmeg
1/2 cup fresh bread crumbs
1 cup heavy cream

- Peel and chop the onion and tomato.

- If you are using fresh parsley, chop it into small pieces.

- Melt the butter in a two-quart saucepan and add the onion.

- Cook over low heat until the onion is soft, stirring it occasionally.

- Add the remaining ingredients except the cream (tomato, parsley, crabmeat, salt, nutmeg, and breadcrumbs).

- Stir and simmer the mixture for five minutes.

- Pour the heavy cream into the saucepan and keep stirring.

- Heat the stew until it bubbles around the edges.

- Remove the stew from the heat and let it cool slightly.

- Serve the stew with bread or rice.

This activity should be done with adult supervision.

Activity
Nine Men's Morris

Today children play many of the same games that were enjoyed in colonial times. Through games, children learned to solve problems and follow directions. Nine Men's Morris is a simple game of skill and logic that colonial children played. You can draw the game diagram on paper, in the dirt, or with sidewalk chalk. The object is to capture the other player's game pieces until he or she has only two left.

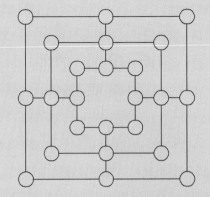

Directions

Large sheet of paper
Pencil or other drawing tool
18 playing pieces of 2 different colors
*Each player gets 9 pieces of
the same color.*
*You can use things like coins,
paper clips, jelly beans, or stones.*

- Draw a game board on paper, using the pattern above. (Colonial children might have drawn the game in the dirt.)
- Give nine playing pieces of the same color to each player.
- Players take turns placing their markers, one at a time, on the circles where the lines cross each other.
- Look for horizontal and vertical cross points. Diagonals do not count.

- Your objective is to place your pieces on three circles in a row that are connected by lines. This is called a "mill."
- Each time you form a mill, you remove one of your opponent's pieces from the board and keep it. You cannot remove a piece from your opponent's mill until all other pieces are removed.
- When all the pieces are on the board, players take turns moving their pieces. You can only move along the lines to an open circle.
- If you form a mill, you remove one of the other player's pieces.
- If you make two mills at once, you can remove two pieces.
- When your opponent has only two pieces left, you win.

This activity should be done with adult supervision.

MARYLAND
Time Line

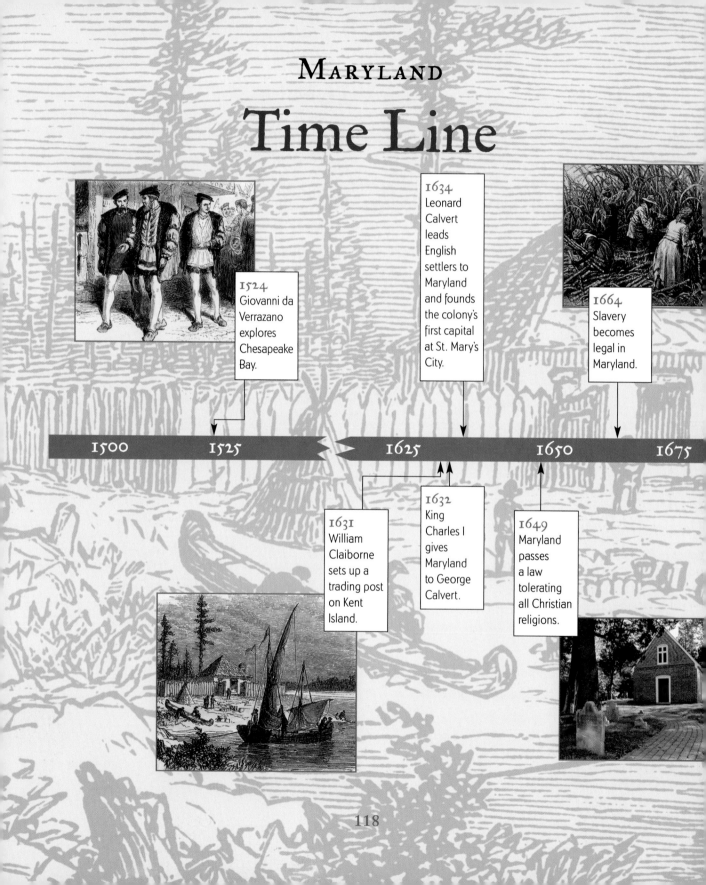

1524 Giovanni da Verrazano explores Chesapeake Bay.

1634 Leonard Calvert leads English settlers to Maryland and founds the colony's first capital at St. Mary's City.

1664 Slavery becomes legal in Maryland.

1500   1525   1625   1650   1675

1631 William Claiborne sets up a trading post on Kent Island.

1632 King Charles I gives Maryland to George Calvert.

1649 Maryland passes a law tolerating all Christian religions.

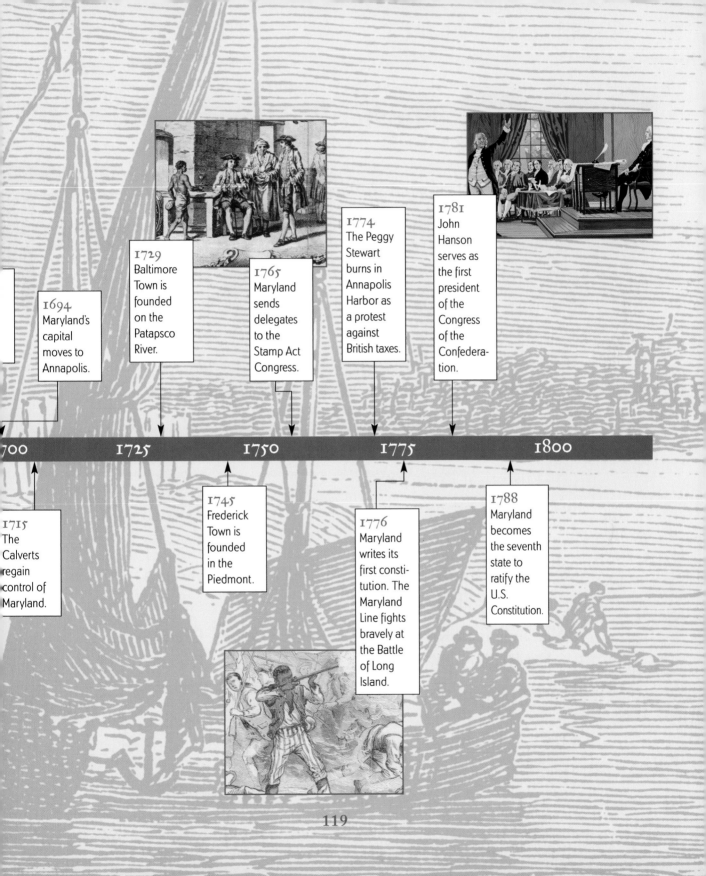

1694
Maryland's capital moves to Annapolis.

1729
Baltimore Town is founded on the Patapsco River.

1765
Maryland sends delegates to the Stamp Act Congress.

1774
The Peggy Stewart burns in Annapolis Harbor as a protest against British taxes.

1781
John Hanson serves as the first president of the Congress of the Confederation.

1715
The Calverts regain control of Maryland.

1745
Frederick Town is founded in the Piedmont.

1776
Maryland writes its first constitution. The Maryland Line fights bravely at the Battle of Long Island.

1788
Maryland becomes the seventh state to ratify the U.S. Constitution.

700   1725   1750   1775   1800

119

Further Reading

Burgan, Michael. *Colonial and Revolutionary Times.* Danbury, CT: Franklin Watts, 2003.

Johnston, Joyce. *Maryland.* Minneapolis, MN: Lerner Publications, 2003.

Lough, Loree. *Lord Baltimore: English Politician and Colonist.* Philadelphia, PA: Chelsea House, 2000.

Schaun, George, and Virginia Schaun. *Everyday Life in Colonial Maryland.* 15th ed. Lanham, MD: Maryland Historical Press, 1980.

Stefoff, Rebecca. *Colonial Life.* New York, NY: Benchmark Books, 2003.

Wilbur, C. Keith. *The Woodland Indians.* Philadelphia, PA: Chelsea House, 1997.

Williams, Jean Kinney. *The Maryland Colony.* Chanhassen, MN: The Child's World, 2004.

Glossary

artisans skilled craftspeople

boycott an organized effort not to buy certain goods

confederacy a group of states or other political units that unite for common defense

consent approval

delegate a representative to a conference or convention

dominate to control or rule; to have power over someone or something

elite the most powerful members of a group or community

expedition a journey for exploration

fertilizer a substance that helps crops grow

freeman someone who arrived in the colonies as a free person, not a slave or indentured servant

immigration moving to a new country to start a new life

investor one who places money in a company to help it grow, hoping to get more money back.

missionaries people who attempt to change the religious beliefs of others to match their own

mulatto a term used in colonial times for a person of mixed racial background

nobility people of high rank or social position

pamphlet a printed document with no cover

Parliament the governing body of Great Britain

peninsula an area of land surrounded by water on three sides

plantation a large farm that often grows just one major crop

preeminence the top position or standing in a group

prejudice hatred or fear of a particular group of people

ratify to approve by a formal agreement

recruit to enroll or enlist someone

repeal to take back or undo

sects small groups that break off from larger churches because of different views on their religion's teachings

smuggle to bring goods into a country illegally

tyrannical acting as a tyrant by denying people their rights and freedom

Index